PROPHECIES
WORLD EVENTS
BY
NOSTRADAMUS

TRANSLATED AND INTERPRETED BY

Stewart Robb

Liveright Publishing Corporation
New York

4/01

By The Same Author

WHAT THE FUTURE HOLDS
NEW NOSTRADAMUS
NOSTRADAMUS ON NAPOLEON, HITLER & THE PRESENT CRISIS

Translations:

Beaumarchais' BARBER OF SEVILLE
Wagner's RING OF THE NIBELUNG

Permission has been obtained from Farrar, Straus and Cudahy, Inc., New York, to quote from *The History of France,* by Andre Maurois; and from G. P. Putnam and Sons, New York, to quote from *Louis Philippe, King of the French,* by Agnes de Stoeckel.

4 5 6 7 8 9 0

PRINTED IN THE UNITED STATES OF AMERICA

Liveright Publishing Corporation, 500 Fifth Avenue, New York, N.Y. 10110

W. W. Norton & Company Ltd., 37 Great Russell Street, London WC1B 3NU

ISBN 0-87140-220-3

CONTENTS

II. PROPHECIES OF DATED EVENTS

III. PROPHECIES OF PERIODS OF TIME

IV. PROPHECIES FULFILLED IN THE 16th AND 17th CENTURIES

V. THE FRENCH REVOLUTION

VI. THE TWENTIETH CENTURY

A WORD TO THE READER

BOOKS on Nostradamus take it for granted that the man was a prophet. I have not taken this for granted, and my prime purpose in this book is to prove that prophecy is a scientific fact.

In his Dedicatory Epistle to Henry the Second, King of France, Nostradamus asseverates of his prophecies, "they have but one sense and one only meaning, and are quite unmingled with calculation that is of ambiguity or amphibology." Interpreters of the seer have not paid sufficient attention to these words. When they come to a quatrain in which there is no mention of a place-name they feel free to interpret the prophecy of England, France, Germany, Italy, Russia, or any other country they may please. But the lines, not being ambiguous — and this means *to the reader* — invariably refer to France, the patriotic prophet's native land. If the prediction speaks of "the king," "the government," or "the nation," the king, government, and nation of France are meant. The interpreter has no right, for instance, to explain "the king" as the king of England.* If Nostradamus means the king of England he is quite capable of saying so — and does.

This method which I use throughout the book may be designated as "interpretation by restriction," and should not prove unsatisfying to the sceptical inquirer, who is constantly saying, "Well, you can apply these prophecies to so many events." Here he will see that the

---

* If Nostradamus were an American and made predictions about "the President," it would be understood that the President of the United States was meant, not, for instance, the President of Brazil.

generalizing mode of interpreting is neither necessary nor correct. And if Nostradamus were not an authentic prophet this method of "interpretation by restriction" would create difficulties for any interpreter.

In the present volume the reader will see that three sections are devoted respectively to most of the quatrains where Nostradamus predicts personal proper names, dates, and periods of time. This method of grouping the prophecies has never been done before and shows them in a particularly powerful light.

My text of the prophet is from Bareste, and Le Pelletier, who have had access to the first extant editions: 1555, 1566, 1568.

BIOGRAPHICAL NOTE

NOSTRADAMUS (Michel de Notredame) was an involuntary prophet, though he wisely cultivated his God-given faculty by prayer and meditation. He was born December 14, 1503 in St. Remy, Provence, France. His father was a very busy and successful notary public. Both parents were of gentle birth. It is said that both a knowledge of mathematics and the faculty of prophecy descended to the son from his mother's progenitors. He was put to school at Avignon "to learn the humanities" and thence to the University of Montpellier to study medicine. Here he took his doctorate, with dazzling speed and success. He soon won extraordinary fame and repute as a doctor, curing thousands in the plague years by unorthodox remedies. Much professional jealousy and malice was thereby directed on him. He settled in Salon, and here it was he first began to prophesy, first modestly publishing almanacs. These were a success. In March, 1555, appeared his first book of prophecies, consisting of a preface to his infant son Cesar, followed by three hundred and fifty-four "quatrains," or four-line verse predictions. This book was called *The True Centuries (Les Vrayes Centuries)*, a "Century" being not a hundred years but a group (book) of one hundred stanzas. His notoriety grew. He was summoned to court by Henry the Second and his wife Catherine de Medici, and there was wonderfully well entertained. His neighbors held him in awe and respect; kings, princes and prelates beat a path to his door; he was never in want. Chavigny writes, "those who came to France sought Nostradamus as the only thing to be seen there." He published more of his verse prophecies, dedicating them to this king. He died in 1566, a prophet with honor in his own country.

9

I

PROPHECIES OF PERSONAL PROPER NAMES

ACHILLES DE HARLAY

The treasure vault cut off by Achilles,
The quadrangle known to posterity;
At the Royal deed the comment will be known,
Body seen hanged in sight of the populace.

L'arc du thresor par Achilles deceu,
Au procrees sceu la quadrangulaire;
Au faict Royal le comment sera sceu,
Corps veu pendu au veu du populaire. (7.1)

UNDER the regency of Marie de Medici, Queen Mother of France, widow of Henry IV and mother of Louis XIII, the Italian Concino Concini and his sorceress wife gained complete control of the state. According to Montgomery, "their ambition and greed knew no bounds. They used the public money to buy estates, offices, and honors for themselves and their relatives. They took bribes from those who wanted government favors, and they got a large revenue by selling pardons to rich criminals. The money which Henry IV had accumulated was wasted by them, and by Marie, in gifts, pensions, and salaries. Still Concini and his friends were not satisfied. Now that they had plundered the royal treasury they wanted political power. It seemed as though their object was to tear France to pieces and divide it among themselves." The States General was called (1614), but nothing was accomplished. The Parlement, France's Supreme Court, played politics. "In their protests, they attacked the Florentine, Concini, as they were later to attack Mazarin whom he resembled." (Bainville) According to Garencieres, Concini, now known as the Marshal d'Ancre — a title he bought — "was first complained of, for his maleversations by Achilles de Harlay, President of Paris."

As a result, "L'arc du thresor" was soon "cut off" (*deceu* has here its original root Latin meaning). The young Louis XIII, listening to his new favorite, an army officer named Albert de Luynes, was quickly turned against the unpopular Marshal D'Ancre. "But the question was how to overturn this all-powerful Florentine, master of the government, the finances, and the army. There was no other resource but boldness." On April 24, 1617, when Concini was entering the quadrangle of the Louvre, he was arrested in the King's name by Vitry, captain of the guards. The unfortunate man made a show of resistance, which was all the captain wanted. Shots rang out from several pistols. The Marshal d'Ancre hadn't a chance. The following day the victim's wife was accused of witchcraft, and shortly after she was beheaded and her body committed to the flames.

The quadrangle would be known to posterity, Nostradamus predicted. The Marshal had not only been slain on the quadrangle but, occording to Patmore, "the body, wrapped in a dirty tablecloth, tied at the head and feet with red ribbons, lay that afternoon in the small tennis court of the palace." No doubt the murder of one of the most powerful men in the kingdom in such a public place would give the scene of the crime a long notoriety.

"At the Royal deed the comment will be known." Sixteen-year old Louis XIII gave the orders for the assassination, and when the good news was brought to him that the deed was done he made a famous comment. "Now I am King!" he exclaimed with gratification, to those who were congratulating him.

"Body seen hanged in the sight of the populace." This too was fulfilled in detail. According to Sir Richard Lodge, "The body of the murdered man was disinterred by the mob, hanged by the feet on the Pont Neuf, dragged in hideous triumph through the streets and finally burnt." A bystander tore out Concini's heart, bit into it, and cried in savage ecstasy, "Ah, that tastes good!"

Observe that Concini's (bought) title, Marshal d'Ancre, seems to have been picked up by the scryer. Marshal d'Ancre means Marshal of the Anchor, and an anchor is certainly an arc.

Here then is a prophecy that becomes utterly lucid when set beside a highly important event in French history, a coup d'etat that brought a figure-head boy monarch to the actuality of rule.

THE GREAT MONTMORENCY AND CLEREPEYNE

The Dauphic Lily will proceed into Nancy
Just as in Flanders elector of the Empire;
New prison for the great Montmorency,
Outside of approved ground delivered to famous punishment.

Le lys Dauffois portera dans Nanci
Jusques en Flandres electeur de l'Empire;
Neufve obturee au grand Montmorency,
Hors lieux prouves delivre a clere peyne. (9.18)

IN 1633 LOUIS XIII (FIRST MONARCH OF THE FLEUR-DE-LYS TO HAVE been a Dauphin since the time of Nostradamus) triumphantly entered Nancy, just as two years later he entered Brussels to rescue the Elector of Trier (Treves), who had been carried off by the Spaniards.

In 1632, a universally beloved hero, the Governor of the Province of Languedoc, known to his contemporaries and to history as the Great Montmorency, was beheaded for rebellion most foul against his monarch. According to Nostradamus the great Montmorency would be delivered to his punishment "outside of approved ground." This detail is historically correct. According to S. H. Hartmann, author of *The Magnificent Montmorency:*

> Almost at the last moment it had been decided to alter the place of execution. It was to take place, not in the Place de Salin before all the people, but in the presence of the essential officials only. The change was represented as a last favour to Montmorency himself, but it is far more probable that Richelieu decided upon it through fear that a public execution might raise some display of popular feeling which

might even culminate in an attempt to rescue the Duke on the very scaffold. Certainly the feeling of the townsfolk was wholly in his favour and during the whole night before the execution the churches had been thronged with sorrowing worshippers.

"Delivered to famous punishment," predicted Nostradamus. The Queen of England pleaded for mercy for the illustrious prisoner. So did the Pope. So did the Duke of Savoy. So did a representative of the Republic of Venice; and there were many others. Louis XIII himself came to Toulouse to witness the trial and execution. He could not move without hearing cries of "Grace! Grace! Misericorde!" Sorrowing murmurs arose all over the province. "These deep feelings were further encouraged by the Church." Special services and public processions on the criminal's behalf were held in all the towns. Toulouse was crammed with 12,000 troops, for fear the people might try to rescue their hero.

Says Nostradamus, *"New prison* for the great Montmorency." Quite so. The repentant prisoner was placed in the newly built Hotel de Ville. Note that *obturee,* here translated as *prison,* is even more accurately rendered as *a place to be closed up in.* The Hotel de Ville was not a prison, but it was used *as* a prison.

After the execution within the closed walls of the courtyard, "men, women and children tore up fragments of the blood-stained pavement to carry away with them as relics. Masses were said for a month, and the whole province mourned for him." Shops everywhere were closed. Many poets dipped their pens in their hearts, and wrote.

A "famous punishment" indeed!

Now turn again to the French text of the prophecy. *"Delivre a clere peyne."* It so happens that the soldier who beheaded Montmorency was named Clerepeyne. This fact is attested to by Etienne Joubert, the Chevalier de Jant, the Cure de Louvicamp, and Motret. The first two named were contemporaries of the event.

As usual, relevancy rules in Nostradamus. All the historical events reported in the quatrain concern rebellion against Louis XIII. Gaston d'Orleans, the king's brother, always reaching for the golden round, had married the pretty daughter of the Duke of Lorraine in Nancy. With his father-in-law's assistance he had raised an army of brigands, fought a battle at Castelnaudary, and lost to the king's troops. Hence the execution of the actively implicated Montmorency. Gaston fled to Flanders and, as he had in Nancy, continued his plots for the overthrow of King and Cardinal. While here in Brussels he was furnished with troops by the Infanta Clara.

Let us tie up the prophetic package again. The three events fore-told took place in 1633, 1635 and 1632 respectively. The time relation-ship therefore is very close. The events are also related, as has been shown, historically. Besides, they are extraordinarily specific, even to details. A city is named and it is stated that a French king who has been a Dauphin will march into it. Then come mention of Flanders and an Elector of the Empire, and we discover historically that the same Dauphin-king who fulfilled the first line of the prophecy by marching into Nancy fulfilled its second line by marching into Flanders to rescue the Elector of the Empire. (The capture by the Spaniards of this same Elector was the *casus belli* between France and Spain.) Then comes by name prophetic mention of the great Montmorency and of his execu-tioner, and the two names stand in that respective relationship to each other. The execution foretold is one of the two most celebrated execu-tions in the century, the other being that of the King of England by Parliament — and that too was predicted by Nostradamus! *(Senat de Londres mettront a mort leur Roy.)*

"THE HEROIC DE VILLARS"

The Tyrrhenian sea, the Ocean by the guard
Of the great Neptune and his trident soldiers.
Provence secure by the hand of the great Tende.
More Mars Narbon the heroic de Villars.

La mer Tyrrhene, l'Occean par la garde
Du grand Neptun & ses tridens soldats.
Provence seur par la main du grand Tende.
Plus Mars Narbon l'heroiq de Vilars. (Presage 2)

"MARSHAL DE VILLARS SAVED FRANCE AT DENAIN," WROTE THAT EX-cellent military authority Napoleon Buonaparte. True; the Marshal de Villars, Comte de Tende, was one of Louis XIV's most valuable as well as valorous generals, worthy of being pitted against even the great Marl-borough. The Marshal's name is a great and glamorous one in the history

"The Heroic de Villars"

books. "Louis XIV had royally supported Villars," writes Maurois. The Sun-King made him Governor of Provence, fulfilling Nostradamus' prediction: "Provence secure by the hand of the great Tende." (Just as an earlier Tende, an ancestor of de Villars, had been granted the governorship of this same province six years after Nostradamus' death. Provence was secure, for Louis XIV believed that all wars should be fought away from home, and he remarked to his great man of war: "Since there must be war, it is better to wage it against my enemies than against my children."

Through "the heroic de Villars," predicted the prophet, Mars Narbon would be even more secure than Provence. Mars Narbo is *Narbo Martius,* Narbonne in the department of l'Aude, "said to be so called from its founder *Martius.* It was here that the French protestants (Camisards) waited for promised help, but quite in vain, after the submission of Jean Cavalier (1704) to Marshal Villars, at a Conference held at Nimes. Louis XIV was so beset by the enemies of France that he sent the Marshal into Languedoc to pacify the districts he despaired of subduing by force." (Ward is here explaining another quatrain which contains a line on the same situation: "Aid Narbon cut off by a conversation.")

The entire quatrain concerns security; security of (1) the waves, (2) Provence, (3) Mars Narbon. Quite an orderly prophecy!

Let us see exactly how well the prophecy and history match.

What was Predicted	What was Fulfilled
"The Tyrrhenian sea, the Ocean by the guard of the great Neptune and his trident soldiers."	Maurois closes a paragraph on de Villar's deeds with mention of Britannia, holder of the trident emblem of sea rule: "England emerged mistress of the waters and at ease on the continent. The days of British dominion were beginning."
	The Tyrrhenian sea is part of the Mediterranean. Sardinia, Sicilia and Corsica overlook it. Now, de Villars, writing autobiographically of the part he played in the Cevennes troubles, says: "The rebels had a respite because I was obliged to repair to the coast, which seemed menaced by a squadron of 45 vessels of the line which

the English had brought into the Mediterranean. I was warned in time and took measures, so that neither the officers that landed nor those sent by the Duke of Savoy could enter the country."

"Provence, secure by the hand of the great Tende."

In 1712, in partial reward for his pacification of the Cevennes and for later deeds Louis XIV made de Villars governor of Provence.

"More Mars Narbon . . ."

De Villars made this Protestant stronghold in the Cevennes very secure indeed by a wise and conciliatory conversation with its Huguenot leader.

". . . the heroic de Villars."

". . . an honorable man of high courage, moral and physical, and a soldier who stands above all his contemporaries and successors in the eighteenth century, on the same height as Marlborough and Frederick." (Encyclopaedia Britannica on de Villars.)

NOSTRADAMUS

NARBON AND SAULCE

(a) "Lincoln in a theater, Booth is the assassin"

If the foregoing hypothetical line had been written by an *American* prophet one hundred years before the event it would stamp him an authentic seer.

(b) "One poet will be called Byron, and Keats . . ."

If the foregoing line had been written by an *English* prophet one hundred years before the event it would stamp him an authentic seer.

(c) "One betrayer will be titled Narbon, and Saulce . . ."

That line was written by a *French* prophet more than two hundred years before the event, and stamps him an authentic seer. The entire prophecy reads:

> The husband, alone, afflicted, will be mitred
> Return, conflict will take place at the Tuileries:
> By five hundred, one betrayer will be titled
> Narbon and Saulce, "we have oil with knives."
>
> *Le part soluz, mary sera mitre*
> *Retour, conflict passera sur le thuille:*
> *Par cinq cents, un trahyr sera tiltre*
> *Narbon et Saulce par coutaux avons d'huille. (9.34)*

Even a reader with no knowledge of French can plainly read in the original text the two names *Narbon* and *Saulce*, whose concurrence in this one prophecy is no less remarkable than would be a similar concurrence of "Lincoln and Booth" or "Byron and Keats." The quatrain is also remarkable for the amount of historical fact packed within it, and for its utter simplicity of expression. It is written in almost basic French. *Part* is Renaissance French for *husband* (*la part* would be *wife*), and *mary* (not *husband*) is an old word for *afflicted*. Both words were common in their time. *Saulce* is the sixteenth century form of *Sauce*. (Cf. *hault* which became *haut*, *chaulx* which became *chaux*, and numerous other examples.)

When Louis XVI and his wife Marie Antoinette made their famous escape from Paris on the night of June 20, 1791, they were successful in getting as far as the town of Varennes. But there they were detained by the mayor Sauce, who invited them into his grocery shop to rest and refresh themselves. Bury relates, "At first Sauce beguiled the king over a battle of wine, and then introduced a travelled fellow townsman who identified him." "Sauce could have saved the king," writes Madame Campan in her memoirs. With tears in her eyes Marie Antoinette pleaded with Madame Sauce to prevail upon her husband to let them continue on their way to the border, but she replied firmly, "I would like to, Your Highness, for I love my king, but I love my husband too and would not have him lose his head." So for the night the royal family were bundled into a room above the grocery shop, and there they were forced to remain till the commissioners from Paris came to carry them back to the sullen, threatening capital. For this manifestation of "civic virtue" and heroism Sauce was praised by the Assembly and voted a reward of 20,000 livres. History relates that the mayor touchingly declared, "I love my king, but I shall remain faithful to my country." Later he was guillotined.

So Sauce was a betrayer, as Nostradamus prophesied he would be. Note too that the name Sauce does not occur again in the pages of universal history!

Soon after the fateful return from Varennes (the word *retour* occurs in the quatrain), the celebrated, underrated Count Narbon "who favored a moderate revolution" (Larousse) was made Louis' Minister of War. Governeur Morris, the American ambassador to France, wrote of him in his Diary of the French Revolution (v. 2, p. 378), "The Assembly is very low and would have been quite down but that Narbonne's intrigues have contributed to give them a little lift at the Expence of Order and good government, in order to feather his Nest. He is well with Brissot and the Rest of that wretched and pernicious faction." Historian Louis Madelin relates that soon the Court accused him of handing over the monarchy to the demagogues . . . the Catholics even went so far as to charge him with 'Protestant intrigues' with Madame de Stael." The queen hated him, and on March 10, 1792, the king dismissed him.

By 1792 the old regime was in the vortex. War was declared on Austria. The first reverses began to frighten the French people, and they angrily demanded that the Assembly immediately depose the suspected Louis. Not satisfied with that, they mobbed the Tuileries. Weber, an eye-witness, writes:

"With a calm heart, sole legacy of an irreproachable life, the king, approaching, saw a door-panel yield to the blow of a pike which barely missed wounding him. Seeing a second panel, hacked to pieces, fall at his feet, he quietly ordered the door opened, and appearing before the rebels said: 'I am your king. What do you want of me?'

"A sudden apparition of divinity in the midst of fire and lightning would not have made a greater impression on this crowd of brigands than that produced by the appearance of the king *alone,* without guards and without attendants."

Ferrieres, another eye-witness, takes up the story: "Legendre arrives. He presents a red cap to the king. One of the four grenadiers pushes it away. 'Let him do what he wants,' the king says: 'he will offer me some rudeness, what of it?' The king takes the red cap and puts it on his head. The people cheer triumphantly."

Duruy writes, "This fatal day inaugurated the Reign of Terror." But the second attack on the Tuileries two months later was more fatal still. On August 10, 1792, the palace was pillaged by a raging mob, the Swis guard massacred, while the royal family fled to the trembling Assembly. Deposition was demanded, obtained, and "third estate became first," as Nostradamus writes elsewhere. The king was committed to the Temple, and five months later, on January 21, 1793, he was led to the guillotine.

The "Narbon, Saulce" quatrain of Nostradamus is a marvelous pen-picture in which even the details are of great significance. Here is the evidence:

Husband: When we think of the last days of Louis XVI we picture him above all as a husband. The tragedy was his separation from his wife and children.

Alone: Had Louis not appeared alone in the midst of the angry mob he would probably have been lynched.

Afflicted: We do not ordinarily associate affliction with a mitring. But this was a peculiar kind of mitring.

Mitred: This accurately describes what actually happened to the king. Ward writes, "The red cap of Liberty was called the Phrygian bonnet or mitre, from its being the headdress of the priests of Mithras ... The god Mithras is depicted on coins in this very cap; further, it furnishes the lively etymology of the word mitre itself. It was for ages, before the French took it up, the received emblem of that frantic crime that has been called Liberty."

Return: The events recorded in this prophecy date from the famous return from Varennes, for which Sauce was responsible.

Tuileries: "Le thuille" means "the place of the tiles." When Nostradamus wrote this prophecy, the site of the Tuileries was only an old tile kiln. The palace was not begun till after the prophet's death.

Five hundred: Five hundred and thirteen Marseillais led the attack on the Tuileries, but historians generally refer to them as "the Five Hundred." Nostradamus' reason for mentioning these men is obvious: as they marched they sang a song now known as the national anthem of France: the world-famous Marseillaise.

"We have oil." This expression may be explained by the following dialogue:

> Customer: Have you any oil?
> Storekeeper: Yes, madame, we have oil.

Had our hypothetical American prophecy read in part: Booth "We act on the stage," it would be no more specific than Nostradamus' association of Sauce with oil-selling. When Louis XVI and Marie Antoinette stopped off at Varennes, Sauce invited them to rest in his grocery store. The queen sat between two piles of candles. Oil cans were suspended from the rafters—for measuring out oil by the quintal. It was in this shop that the queen pleaded with Madame Sauce. It was directly above it that the royal family were lodged for the night. In his biography of Marie Antoinette, Stefan Zweig comments on the smell of rancid oil in Sauce's shop. So the line, "Sauce, 'we have oil.' " is powerfully prophetic.

There is even more meaning in it: Sauce was of the bourgeoisie. Narbon was of the nobility. "One betrayer will be *titled*." Nostradamus is showing how Louis was betrayed on all sides, by the whole nation. All were against him, the people, as evidenced by the two attacks on the Tuileries; the nobility, as represented by titled Narbon; and the bourgeoisie—Sauce the oil-seller.

All the events related in this marvelous quatrain took place between June 21, 1791 and March 10, 1792, this is, within a period of a little less than eleven months. The names Narbon and Sauce have no historical significance as betrayers except *within this time*. "Return" and "Sauce" are directly related; the grocer-mayor was responsible for the king's capture, and if it had not been for this event the mitring of Louis and the conflict at the Tuileries could not have taken place. Everything recorded in the prophecy depicts the downfall of the old regime in the person of Louis XVI. Certainly it would be hard to pack more history into four lines, and it is impossible to read more than one meaning into them.

GORSAS AND NARBON

> Gorsan, Narbonne, by the salt will warn,
> Tuching pardon, Parpignan betrayed,
> The red city will not wish to consent to it,
> By high Flight grey drape life failed.

> *Gorsan, Narbonne, par le sel advertir,*
> *Tucham la grace, Parpignan trahie,*
> *La ville rouge n'y voudra consentir,*
> *Par haulte Vol drap gris vie faillie.* (8.22)

THIS PROPHECY SHOULD BE READ AND STUDIED WITH THE NARBON-SAULCE quatrain. The connecting link is of course Narbon. Each of the quatrains contains, besides the connecting name, the name of an important figure in the Revolution, and each of these two names, Gorsas, Saulce, occurs only once in history, and both occur at the same time. Saulce detained the King in Varennes, and Gorsas (Gorsan and Gorsas are almost identical in French) did his journalistic bit for the "red city" and against the legitimate regime.

According to Larmor. *Parpignan* here stands for, not the city of Perpignan, of which it is a deliberate mis-spelling, but for Paris-born. *Pignus*, however, in the Latin means "pledge," not "born," and Paris-pledge stands well for the hostage-prisoner King. Larmor states that Gorsas and Narbon, pitying their monarch, warned him of a possible pardon by a message hidden in a salt-shaker. There seems no historical evidence to support the story, though this kind of thing happened with the royal family. In fact once a suspicious commissioner broke open peach-pits to see if they contained secret messages for the queen.

Gorsas, though a revolutionist, was not a bad fellow. On that unholy day when the Swiss guard were massacred he pled hard "with infuriated groups." And according to Carlyle:

> He stole, afterwards, in August, to Paris; lurked several weeks about the Palais *ci-devant* Royal! was seen there, one day; was clutched, identified, and without ceremony, being already 'out of the Law,' was sent to the Place de la Revolution. He died, recommending his wife and children to the pity of the Republic. It is the ninth day of October 1793. Gorsas is the first Deputy that dies on the scaffold; he will not be the last.

The Red City did not want to consent to any pardon for the betrayed "Paris-pledge." The king had fled, therefore he was a traitor worthy of death. It was a "high flight" indeed, that of the "grey drape," and as a result his "life failed." There would be a flight by night, predicted Nostradamus elsewhere, through a forest, to Varennes, by a "monk-king in grey;" and "elected cap." or elected Capet, the caped one would "cause tempest, fire, blood, slice." (See page 98) And the good Bourbon, said the seer, "by flight will unjustly receive his punishment." (See page 90) Observe the everlasting internal relationship of the prophecies under scrutiny, a relationship impossible if chance-begotten.

THE MONTAGNARD AMAR

A QUATRAIN PREDICTING BOTH A NAME AND A DATE

From the mont Aymar the noble will be obscured,
The evil will come at the juncture of Saone & Rhone,
Soldiers hidden in the woods day of Lucy,
When there was never so horrible a throne.

Du mont Aymar sera noble obscurcie,
Le mal viendra au joinct de Saone & Rhosne,
Dans bois cachez soldats jour de Lucie,
Que ne fut onc un si horrible throsne. (9.68)

HERE IS A QUATRAIN CROWDED WITH REVOLUTIONARY HISTORY. THE
period predicted is that of the most "horrible throne." Certainly, help-
less Louis XVI found it a most horrible throne to sit on. And when
it was usurped by a bloody Commune, a triumvirate of tyrants, and
twelve reds, and after that — if this could to be topped — by Napoleon, the French throne became the most horrible in history.

The evil came both at and to "the juncture of the Saone and
Rhone." For the juncture is Lyons, "center of republicanism" verging
on the Dauphine — "Cradle of the Revolution" — and later a city
nearly wiped off the map, where the condemned were blown from
the mouths of cannon. Did not the Committee of Public Safety ("the
twelve reds" Nostradamus predicted would rule) decree, in Articles
Three to Five of their bloody document:

THE CITY OF LYONS SHALL BE DESTROYED ...
THE NAME OF LYONS SHALL BE EFFACED FROM THE
LIST OF CITIES OF THE REPUBLIC. THE COLLECTION
OF HOUSES LEFT STANDING SHALL HENCEFORTH
BEAR THE NAME OF VILLE-AFFRANCHIE—THE LIBER-
ATED CITY.

ON THE RUINS OF LYONS SHALL BE RAISED A
COLUMN ATTESTING TO POSTERITY THE CRIMES AND

THE PUNISHMENT OF THE ROYALISTS OF THE CITY,
WITH THIS INSCRIPTION:

LYONS MADE WAR ON LIBERTY.

LYONS IS NO MORE.

18th day of the first month of the Year Two
of the French Republic, One and Indivisible.

The evil was perpetrated by *la Montagne*, or "the Mountain."
Those extreme and bloody reds were so named because they occupied
the upper seats in the Assembly. Amar was one. Amar and Aymar are
the same name. Nostradamus calls him *mont Aymar*, that is, the
Montagnard Amar. As a regicide he helped obscure the most noble
one of all, his lawful Louis. Because of the obscuring of this same
noble one a might rebellion broke out in La Vendee. The iniquity of
this rebellion was denounced by the Montagnard Amar, speaker for
the Committee of Twelve ruling France.

According to Guizot, in the Vendean revolt, Larochejacquelein,
the Catholic aristocrat general "signalized himself by many heroic acts
and gained success against the republicans for some time, but was finally
defeated December 13th, 1793, and escaped with difficulty." The
Vendean peasantry, thanks to the nature of their terrain, were able to
do superb guerilla fighting. They are known to history as *Soldiers of
the Bocage*, that is, woodland fighters. "Their army was singularly
favored by the nature of the country in which it operated," states the
Cambridge History. "Of the three hundred thousand inhabitants of
the Vendee, some seventy five percent were scattered in small villages
through a roadless labyrinth of rough hills and narrow valleys called
the Bocage. It was an ideal country for guerilla fighting, and almost
impossible for scientific warfare." "The Vendean troops, disappearing
like water into the ground, would slip away by all the loopholes known
to themselves alone." "Soldiers hidden in the woods," predicts Nostradamus, and then, pinpointing something in relation to this, he adds:
"day of Lucy." The Day of St. Lucy is December 13. A day of fate.
On it was fought, with most tragic consequences for the soldiers of La
Vendee, the battle of Le Mans. This was the day that broke the back
of the mightiest insurrection the Red Republic had ever known.

Nostradamus is most precise. Not only was the entire Vendean
insurrection one of "soldiers hidden in the woods," but particularly

was it so *on this day*. According to Baron de Barante, a Vendean historian:

> M. de Rochejaquelein tried to defend the approaches of the city, and succeeded for some hours *in a fir wood* which crosses the road. But he no longer found his brave faithful Vendeans with him.

So the soldiers hidden in the wood lost disastrously:

> Doubling eastwards in the hope of effecting a crossing at Saumur or Tours, the *grande armee*, reduced now to some 25,000 broken men, was overtaken at Le Mans by Kleber, Marceau, and Westermann. A bloody victory was followed by a wanton butchery of prisoners; 15,000 persons are said to have perished in this terrible affair (December 13).

> *Cambridge History*

"Soldiers hidden in the woods — day of Lucy — most horrible throne."

Like the rest of the quatrains of Nostradamus, the one under scrutiny forms a tight-knit unity. An important regicide, Amar, is named, he is an obscurer of "the noble one," his political persuasion is indicated; the period is correctly characterized as that of France's "most horrible throne," Lyons is pinpointed for much evil, the date of the crucial battle of Le Mans is given and tied up with "soldiers hidden in the woods," words which fully characterize the nature of the revolt in general and the battle in particular. Then, to return full circle, the same *mont Aymar*, while Spokesman for the Twelve Reds who were guiding the suppression of the insurrection, taxed the Girondins, now rebels against the Montagnards, with inspiring the revolt of the "soldiers hidden in the woods."

With the *Aymar — horrible throne* quatrain should be read another which also mentions "the most horrible throne."

> Great cornerstone will die three leagues from the Rhone;
> Two afflicted close-kinsmen, flee tumult:
> For Mars will make the most horrible throne
> Of Cock, and of Eagle, of France Brothers three.
>
> *Pol mensole mourra trois lieues du Rosne;*
> *Fuis les deux prochains tarasc destrois:*

Car Mars fera le plus horrible trosne
De Coq, et d'Aigle, de France Freres trois. (8.46)

The two prophecies may be read as one, since there cannot be two periods in French history, each of which is *the* most horrible. If Nostradamus were a guesser, to read two or more of his quatrains together because of internal coincidences would ruin any attempt to prove his verses prophetic. But when the prophecies *are* brought together and hooked to one another by their internal links they cast light on one another and are seen and recognized for what they are: *Vrayes Centuries.*

The first line, then, of the quatrain under consideration, was fulfilled when the Rock of Christ's Church was carried captive by Napoleon's men to Valence, where he died. Valence is a town by the Rhone. "Three leagues" means "near," — unless the prophet was three leagues out when he scryed the fate of the Pontiff. Certain it is, though, that Pius VI was the only Pope in history to die near the Rhone River. Admit it, — what is the likelihood that a Pontiff of Rome will die in France? So the first line *alone* of this prophecy forecasts an event unique in history and then places that event correctly in the period of France's Revolutionary fury.

"You two afflicted close-kinsmen, flee tumult!" urges the prophet ironically. Note the French for *close-kinsmen.* Specifically, *prochains* means kinsmen who partake in a heritage. The throne Louis' two brothers fled was their heritage, and later they came to it.

What made the throne so horrible the *prochains* had to flee was its occupancy for the first time by the Cock, emblem of the French people stamped on the coins of the Republic, and then its occupancy (also for the first time) by the Eagle, the son of the Revolution. Strange that all these things should *be* just at that rare time when France has three Brother Rulers.

And also when Pius VI dies near the Rhone River.

So we have fulfilled in *one* concise prophecy:

    (a) Three brothers on the throne of France.
    (b) Likewise the Cock.
    (c) Likewise the Eagle.
    (d) This is the time of France's "most horrible throne."
    (e) The Pope of Rome dies near the Rhone River.
    (f) He dies near the Rhone because of "the most horrible throne."

The Dauphin and Simon the Shoemaker
"They will deny life to the Queen's son."

To predict all these events in one prophecy is beyond the reach of chance. Note too that the various facts correctly prophesied are closely inter-related, cast light on one another, and are highlights of history, — and also tie up with another set of equally remarkable fulfilled facts in the *Aymar* prophecy.

THE YOUNGER LOUIS

His hand in a scarf & his leg bandaged,
The younger Louis will leave the palace,
At the watchword his death will be delayed,
Then he will bleed in the Temple at Easter.

La main escharpe & la jambe bandee,
Louis puisne de palais partira,
Au mot du guet la mort sera tardee,
Puis dans le temple a Pasques saignera. (8.45)

THE COBBLER SIMON MAY NOT HAVE BEEN QUITE AS BRUTAL AS SOME of the Royalist historians of France depict him, but it is known that more than once he whipped the Dauphin too severely. On one occasion young Louis' leg was injured by blows, and on another one of his eyes. Whether the boy ever had to go around with his arm in a sling and his leg bandaged there seems to be no record, but much mystery surrounds the last days of the young heir to the throne of France. Did he bleed at Easter? Again we do not know. Some historians contend that he died June 8, 1795 in his eleventh year as a result of neglect, but others are less certain, thinking he may have been smuggled out of the Temple alive. At any rate there mushroomed thirty odd pretenders to the throne. Still, his death in the Temple is likely.

This prophecy ties up with the quatrain interpreted on page 111 which predicts that *life will be denied* to the son of a queen who is "sent to death by jurors chosen by lot" — statements applicable to no one but Marie Antoinette and the Dauphin — and since the present prophecy involves a younger Louis, wounded, in the Temple, and whose death is delayed, it would seem that the prophecy fits none but this same Louis XVII, titular head of France.

Senart, procurer of the Commune, records that when Simon asked for instructions about the Dauphin under his care, he said to the cobbler:

"What do you decide about the wolf-cub?"

"I shall be able to humble him. So much the worse if he breaks out. I am not answerable for it. After all what do you want? To transport him?"

"No."

"To kill him?"

"No."

"To poison him?"

"No."

"What then?"

"To get rid of him." Translated by Buckley this means: "Thou shalt not kill yet needest not strive officiously to keep alive."

Shortly after this conversation the Dauphin was taken from his mother and kept in an isolated cell. There has been much speculation as to what happened to him, but some mysteries have been cleared up by Louis Hastier.

According to Harmand, who inspected the Dauphin on the 19th of December, 1794, the boy had two tumors on his arm, and swellings on both knees and at the back of the knees. In 1795, when Achille Sevestre formally announced his death to the Convention, on behalf of the Committee of General Security, he stated: "Citizens, for some time the son of Capet has been inconvenienced by a swelling on the right knee and the left wrist; on the 15th Floreal (4th of May) the pains increased ... The doctors' bulletin of yesterday at 11 A.M. announced disquieting symptoms for the life of the patient, and at a quarter past two in the afternoon we received the news of the death of the son of Capet." J. .B Morton states that the Dauphin's "sores had been bathed and dressed." If so, it is more than probable that they were bandaged, as Nostradamus predicts.

"The younger Louis . . . will bleed," says the prophet. This too came true. Beauchesne observes that "A blood-stained sheet covered his remains . . . The sheet being removed, the victim was seen by the new commissaries, bearing the traces left by the professional men; the scalpel of science had mutilated that body."

A strange occurence took place just before the boy's death. Gomin, his attendant, relates that the Dauphin said he could hear the most beautiful music. "Don't you hear it?" he asked. Gomin, thinking the boy's run-down condition responsible for a hallucination, humored him and pretended he could hear the music too. Then the Dauphin heard other sounds: a multitude of voices, from amongst which he could distinguish that of his mother.

PHILIP, CHIEF OF ORLEANS

By avarice, by force & violence
Chief of Orleans will come to vex his own,
Near Saint Memire assault & resistance
Dead in his tent, it will be said that he is sleeping there.

Par avarice, force & violence
Viendra vexer les siens chef d'Orleans,
Pres Sainct Memire assaut & resistance
Mort dans sa tente, diront qu'il dort leans. (8.42)

LOUIS PHILIPPE BECAME "KING OF THE FRENCH" IN JULY, 1830, after rebellion had sent stiff-necked Charles X packing. But after a rule of seventeen years (See page 74), the latter half of which displeased even his supporters by its abuse of power, Louis in turn was given the same treatment. The rebellion that overthrew him was centered around the Cloister of St. Meri, so Nostradamus either heard the name imperfectly or was anagrammatizing it.

The prophet puns rhymingly on the name of his King to be: *Orleans — dort leans*. Comments Laver: "The pun on Orleans would be tiresome in a historian. It is stupefying in Nostradamus, seeing that when he wrote, the whole idea of Orleans would have been completely incomprehensible. Gaston d'Orleans, the founder of the House, was the brother of Louis XIII."

Philip of Orleans did not die of the rebellion, but he almost slept through it. Agnes de Stoeckel, his biographer, writes of the ousting:

The monarch was still sleeping. The King's valet Thuret met them (Thiers and Odillon) to ask if they could wait a little, as his Majesty had looked so dreadfully ill when he had helped him to bed . . . Reluctantly the man left them and went to awaken his master.

1850

Honore Daumier

Louis Philippe
*"By avarice, force and violence chief of Orleans
will come to vex his own."*

In a few minutes Louis Philippe appeared, in his nightshirt, a nightcap on his head.

"Accept my resignation from your Cabinet."

Saying this the King left the room . . .

All that morning, Louis Philippe sat in his cabinet by the fire. People came in and went out, but he did not even see them. His eyes were closed, yet he did not sleep. One of his ex-Ministers asked him: "What does your Majesty intend doing?"

"Nothing. I am defeated."

———

The early dawn of 25th February did not awaken the exhausted King. For the first time for what seemed a century, his sleep was enveloped in silence. Even the rain had ceased. Louis Philippe slept at last, tranquil in the belief that his grandson reigned King of the French . . .

The King beckoned the Sous-Prefet of Dreux to approach the bed. As he did so the Sous-Prefet could scarcely refrain from an exclamation. Could this be the King! The unshaved beard, yesterday's soiled and crumpled shirt, the untidy bed — all spoke of defeat.

"It will be said that he is sleeping there," states the prophecy.

A worse King could have been thrown out. His greatest vice seems to have been one mentioned by the prophet, — "avarice." Agnes de Stoeckel writes:

He had one great weakness; a passion which dominated all others — his pride of his wealth.

Since his return to France in 1815, he had striven ceaselessly to increase his fortune, disputing claims in the Law Courts, poring over his household accounts, watching over his estates with the care of a lover, even pestering his neighbors at Neuily to sell him their lands, so that he could extend his already vast domains.

One of his meanest demonstrations of avarice was when, in a plot with Madame de Feucheres, he engaged her to put pressure on her old lover, the Prince de Conde, to revise his will in favor of the Duc d'Aumale, Louis Philippe's seventh son.

FERDINAND LEAVES THE FLOWER

And Ferdinand blond will be stripped bare,
To leave the flower, to follow the Macedonian,
In great need his route will fail,
And he will march against the Myrmidon.

Et Ferdinand blond sera descorte,
Quitter la fleur, suyvre le Macedon,
Au grand Besoing defaillira sa routte,
Et marchera contre le Myrmidon. (9.35)

OF CZAR FERDINAND OF BULGARIA MONSIEUR ALEXANDRE HEPP, HIS
enthusiastic biographer wrote: "It is a Prince entirely French, by
tradition, by instinct, by aspiration, and by talent, who was the
founder of Bulgaria, and is today its King."

The French had taken him to their hearts. After all, he had
been brought up in France, his mother was a daughter of Louis Phillipe,
King of the French, and in all his actions Ferdinand seemed not only
French but a patriot. When his mother lay awaiting burial, he unbut-
toned his waistcoat to the Duc de Luynes. "There next his heart blazed
the broad red ribbon of the French Legion of Honour, once worn by
Louis Philippe himself." (Hepp)

Hepp, like most of his people, was completely won over by
Ferdinand. In his biography he writes of a little incident that convinced him (if he needed convincing) what a patriot his hero was.
"Seated opposite Ferdinand in the midst of all this azure pomp, the
writer was suddenly brought face to face with a fresh emotion. On
every fork and spoon, on every piece of the massive silver plate was
engraved the French fleur-de-lys. They marked the descent of the
Bulgarian royal couple; the prince as grandson of Louis Philippe,
the Princess Marie Louise as granddaughter of Charles X."

He was set up as Czar of Bulgaria with a substantially French
court and in many other ways he was helped by the generous French
people. According to the anonymous British author of *Ferdinand of
Bulgaria,* published in 1916, in the midst of World War I: "To reor-
ganize the Bulgarian Army he went to France, and there borrowed
money, equipment and military advisers. The French artillery enabled
the Bulgarians to score so heavily over the Turks in their first en-
counters . . . The Bulgarian Black Sea fleet was of French organization,
and its first admiral was a French naval officer named Pichon."

It was not long before Ferdinand decided to give his Army and

Navy some exercise. Turkey was in trouble from within, with young and advanced revolutionists, and from without, having been under attack by both the Albanians and Italians. Now was the time for Ferdinand to save his fellow Christians the Macedonians from the Infidel. The Czar of Bulgaria may have been more or less sincere in this. According to Professor Monroe, 'The majority of the inhabitants of Macedonia are Bulgarians." And according to Lady Grogan, writing in 1918: "The peasantry of Macedonia believe themselves to be Bulgarians; they are Bulgarians in type, customs, language, dress, and tradition. That they were Bulgarians was never questioned by travellers who described and mapped the country before the era of national propaganda began."

After the first Balkan War (1912), waged victoriously by Bulgaria, Greece, Serbia and Montenegro against the Turk, trouble arose over the division of the spoils, and Bulgaria, who found she was not to get Macedonia, which was the main reason for all her fighting, launched a surprise attack on all her allies. According to A. T. Christoff, in *The Truth About Bulgaria*, 1919: "Bulgaria went into the war for the liberation of her own people in Macedonia, who suffered more under Servian and Greek oppression than under the bloody regime of Sultan Hamid." James D. Bourchier, in *International Review*, July, 1919, states: "In all the regions annexed by the Three Powers a process of extermination of the Bulgarian element was carried out."

Whether righteously or not, Bulgaria was soon defeated by her former allies and Ferdinand was forced to sign the humiliating Treaty of Bucharest. Says Schevill:

> All his neighbors had got something substantial, even Rumania, which had not taken up arms against the Turks. And Bulgaria was the poorer by a substantial slice of territory extorted from Ferdinand by his Rumanian neighbours. The Turks had regained possession of Macedonia, including the city of Adrianople. The Greeks had the coveted ports of Salonica and Kavala on the Aegean. The Serbians had Thrace, and a long railway line from Belgrade through Uskub, with an outlet through Greek territory to Salonica.

But Ferdinand persisted in his determination to rescue his blood-brothers, though this would bring more disaster upon himself and near disaster to the Allies in looming World War I. "To leave the flower, to follow the Macedonian," predicted Nostradamus. And so Ferdinand did.

Macedonia was the main bait Germany dangled in front of Ferdinand to bring him into the War on her side. The Allies apparently knew nothing of the offer and suspected nothing. The editor of *The World's Work* explains, "The story of the Bulgarian nation supplied the reason for assuming that Bulgaria's sympathies would inevitably go with the entente." "His traditional friendship with France, and the deep obligation of Bulgaria to Russia and Great Britain, caused the Allied Powers to regard the situation with some complacency."

The anonymous author of *Ferdinand of Bulgaria* says,

> Yes, France felt very sure of Ferdinand . . . His perfidy was not suspected till nearly the end of 1914 when M. Joseph Reinach . . . began to form suspicions. He framed a letter to Ferdinand on February 11, 1915, to the effect that he had to express the uneasiness he was feeling, and which all the French friends of Bulgaria and its Czar felt at recent news.
>
> Ferdinand, in a letter signed "The Good European," his usual signature in this correspondence, told him not to believe the news, adding, "My sentiments remain unchanged." Even then he was bargaining with the enemies of France to betray the cause of the Entente and of the small nations.
>
> The Bulgarian treaty with Germany was signed on July 17, but on August 15 Ferdinand's Minister, M. Dobrovitch, was writing to Paris expressing false hopes of a future Russian success, and holding out elusive promises that Bulgaria would intervene on the side of the Allies.
>
> Radoslavoff, the prime minister of Bulgaria, declared: "We will fight but for one end, that is to extend our frontiers until they embrace the people of our own blood, but that end must be assured us beyond all doubt. If we are asked to fight alone, we are ready. If we are asked to fight with Greece, Servia and Rumania, in a new Balkan Alliance on the side of the Allies, we say: Give us back our Macedonia, and we will fight in the way we can serve you best."

But it was too late, for Bulgaria took as true coin Germany's offer of the sun, moon and Macedonia.

"Ferdinand . . . will march against the Myrmidon," says Nostradamus. Any student of classical literature knows that the Myrmidons are Thracian soldiers. Now this is precisely what Ferdinand did, twice. In the first Balkan War, states the author of *Ferdinand of Bulgaria*, Bulgaria's "whole pretext for interference was supplied by the oppression of the Christian nations in Thrace, Macedonia and Albania by the minions of the Red Sultan." At the close of the Balkan War the spoils of Thrace went to Serbia. And in World War I, which began by a declaration of war upon *Serbia* by Austria-Hungary, Bulgaria's entry into the conflict automatically brought her into conflict with Thrace. So Nostradamus' prophecy was most literally fulfilled when Ferdinand found himself fighting the Myrmidon.

Bulgaria had been 'stripped bare" in punishment for her aggressive part in Balkan War II, but her punishment was to be repeated with interest at the close of World War I. Robert Ergang says:

> Of all the conquered states Bulgaria was treated most severely at Paris . . . The Allies made the Bulgarians pay heavily for Ferdinand's bad choice, leaving them only an area of some 30,000 square miles with a population of less than five millions. A reparations burden of 2.25 billion gold francs was also forced on the weary shoulders of a country which had been almost continuously at war since 1912. As early at 1923 the indemnity was reduced to about one fourth of the original sum, but the load was still too heavy for a war-weakened land. Resentment against the king was so great that he fled the country in 1918 and was succeeded by his son, King Boris III.

With this stripping the *Ferdinand* prophecy of Nostradamus was finally fulfilled. For the sake of completeness in the interpretation, however, it should be mentioned that the prophet apparently made a little slip-up. From the pictures I have seen of King Ferdinand of Bulgaria he was brunette. It seems then that Nostradamus got the color of his hair wrong.

FRANCO

A REMARKABLE PROPHECY OF NOSTRADAMUS ON THE World War II is one which enabled me to make a forecast of astonishing precision. I fully interpreted the prophecy in my *Nostradamus on Napoleon, Hitler and the Present Crisis* (Scribner) and also in *What the Future Holds* (Booktab). The French seer actually names the present Spanish *caudillo*:

> The assembly will go out from the castle of Franco,
> The ambassador not satisfied will make a schism:
> Those of the Riviera will be involved,
> And they will deny the entry to the great gulf.

> *De castel Franco sortira l'assemblee,*
> *L'ambassadeur non plaissant fera scisme:*
> *Ceux de Riviere seront en la meslee,*
> *Et au grand goulphre desnieront l'entree.* (9.16)

By means of a correct reading of this extremely lucid prophecy I was able to forecast: that Generalissimo Franco would meet the Axis powers on the Riviera, that there would be a crucial meeting, and that Hitler and Mussolini would fail to get Gibraltar. For several months before the event I carefully scanned the front pages of the newspapers, in the expectation that such a meeting would take place. It did, on February 13, 1941. The *New York Times* headlined *Riviera*. Most of our columnists and commentators believed the Axis talks would result in Axis success, but I confidently awaited a contrary outcome, and was justified. In my Scribner *Nostradamus*, published October, 1941, I asseverated, interpreting this prophecy, "After the war, history books summarizing the part played by Spain in the present conflict will mention that Franco met Mussolini on the Riviera, and refused to co-operate with the Axis to let troops pass through Spain to Gibraltar." Even this was going very much out on a limb, and nearly four years before the end of the war, for was not Hitler believed to be strong enough to falsify such a forecast at any moment? But Der Fuehrer never reached Gibraltar.

Note too how the Franco prophecy points in the direction of an allied victory, for had Hitler been going to win he would have obtained the rock and anything else he wanted.

The odds against this prediction being a chance coincidence are very high. Together with the name Franco — which occurs only once in the writings of the prophet — there is mentioned the Riviera and the denial of entry to the great gulf. To a Frenchman the great gulf is the gulf of the Mediterranean and its entry is most certainly at Gibraltar.

If mention of the Riviera is but a happy hit, it is one of extremely remote possibility. The map of Europe is dotted with thousands of place-names. The odds against naming the Riviera together with Franco are equal in number to the number of European place-names it is possible to mention. Working on a basis of chance one name would be likely to be as significant as another. Yet the Riviera is the very name that is significant *above all others*. However, for the sake of the sceptic let us reduce the odds to a thousand — though obviously they are much greater.

The last line may be treated in the same manner. The conclusion of the meeting is correctly and precisely stated. Ask the question, "In how many ways may a meeting conclude?" Thousands — putting it mildly! Yet for the sceptic's sake we again reduce the odds to a thousand.

Result: one chance in a million (1000 x 1000) that the naming of Franco is merely a happy hit. Actually the odds against its being so defy calculation.

PAU. NAY. LORON—NAPOLEON

Pau. nay. loron will be more fire than blood,
To swim in praise, the great one to flee on the confluence of waters,
He will refuse the agassas entry,
Great bridge Durance he will hold them imprisoned.

Pau. nay. loron plus feu qu'a sang sera,
Laude nager, fuir grand aux surrez,
Les agassas entree refusera,
Pampon Durance, les tiendra enserrez. (8.1)

THIS PROPHECY IS TREATED AT LENGTH IN NOSTRADAMUS ON NAPOLEON,
so the salient historical facts it predicted will only be summarized
here. Pau. nay. loron is more of fire than blood, that is, he is more
a men of war than a king (though he was of noble birth too). His sea-
flight from Elba is famous in history. He held the two Piuses, VI and
VII, prisoner in France, refusing them entry into their Papal States.
(Agassas, Greek for *magpies*, in French is pie, which also means Pius.)
The two *pie* were held prisoner in Valence and Grenoble respectively,
in that south east section of France through which runs the River
Durance.

Pau. nay. loron (note the periods) is an anagram. Separate from
it *roy*, which leaves Pau. na. lon, then reverse, and you have

Na. pau. lon.

If this decoding were merely a lucky hit, and thereby a twisting of
the letters (though one can only *un*-twist what is clearly an anagram)
still the odds against such a possibility are practically incalculable. The
reader may judge of this for himself by experiment. Let him take down
a book from his shelf, open it at the beginning, pencil-mark off the
text into groups of eleven letters apiece, and continue doing this till he
finds a combination re-arrangeable to Napaulon roy. And if after weary
months the reader ever does chance upon a group of eleven letters so
decodable his troubles are only beginning, because the syllables of the
Emperor's name are intact, as removal of roy shows, leaving Pau.na.lon.
If the Frenchman Nostradamus, prophesying on the kings of France,
were working only by chance, the odds against his hitting off in an
anagram the name of one of his own rulers would be as great as those
encountered by the reader conducting this experiment.

Yet this anagram is but a small fragment of a quatrain in which
everything else as well points to the French man of fire and blood.

"PAU. NAY. LORON"

THE THREE HISTER QUATRAINS—HITLER

Liberty will not be recovered,
A bold, black, base-born, iniquitous man will occupy it;
When the material of the bridge is completed,
The republic of Venice will be annoyed by Hister.

La liberte ne sera recouvree,
L'occupera noir, fier, vilain, inique,
Quand la matiere du pont sera ouvree,
D'Hister, Venise faschee la republique. (5.29)

"Hister" is an old, old name for the Danube, old even when Nostradamus resucitated it for some good reason of his own. But the passage of the centuries has brought it up to date. It was the obvious word for the prophet to use. It meant the Danube: it also served as an anagram of Hitler. An anagram is a proper name with its letters rearranged. In the sixteenth century when Nostradamus wrote, anagrams were as popular as crossword puzzles are today. Now *Hister* with one letter changed will give *Hitler*. The change of one letter was permissible in anagram writing (see *Dictionnaire de Trevoux*). What other word could serve better than *Hister* to specify both the name, and the place of origin of "the bold, black, base-born, iniquitous man" who was to "occupy liberty"?

The Material of the Bridge

What bridge? There is no need to conjecture. Look into the quatrain for the answer. Only one river is mentioned: the Danube. So the bridge should be the bridge over the Danube. Such a bridge was headlined on the front-page in our newspapers on February 21, 1941. I had actually been watching for mention of it daily on the front pages.

In the N. Y. Herald Tribune:

> SOFIA REPORTS
> NAZI BRIDGE
> OVER DANUBE

The article explained clearly why Nostradamus wrote:

When the *material* of the bridge is *completed*

instead of

> When the bridge is built

"The Germans, a report from Sofia said, had *completed a pontoon* bridge across the Danube near Giurgiu, Rumania, to Bulgaria."

And

> "When the material of the bridge is completed,
> The republic of Venice will be annoyed by Hister."

By synecdoche, "republic of Venice" stands for Italy. (Also the line has an ironical ring to it, with overtones of Hitler's opposition to democracy.) The meaning of the last two lines must then be: "When the pontoon bridge is completed over the Danube Italy will be annoyed by Hitler." Exactly so! Within a month of the building of this bridge our newspapers began to feature articles on German infiltration into the land of the Duce.

> In place quite near, but far from Venus,
> The two greatest of Asia, and Africa
> It will be said that they are from the Rhine and Hister,
> Cries, tears at Malta, and Ligurian coast.

> *En lieu bien proche esloigne de Venus,*
> *Les deux plus grands de l'Asie et d'Aphrique*
> *Du Rhin et Hister qu'on dire sont venus,*
> *Cris, pleurs a Malte, et coste ligustique.* (4.68)

This quatrain is one I do not find too clear. There were tears at Malta and in Italy (Ligurian coast); but the relationship of even this part of the prediction to the rest is not easy to determine.

> Animals ferocious with hunger to swim rivers:
> Greater part of the camp will be against Hister,
> It will have the great man carried in an iron cage,
> When the German child watches the Rhine.

> *Bestes farouches de faim fleuves tranner:*
> *Plus part du camp encontre Hister sera,*
> *En caige de fer le grand fera treisner,*
> *Quand Rin enfant Germain observera.* (2.24)

Although I quoted this prophecy in my book on Nostradamus, I did not then gather the significance of the iron cage. It had been

From a contemporary cartoon in *The Glasgow Bulletin*

Shade of Napoleon: "I'd just like to say my mistake was not knowing when to stop."

suggested to me though that the reference was to a submarine. If so, the quatrain would apparently mean that when only young Germans were left to watch the Rhine the majority of Hitler's officers would be against his policies and that at this time it would have him carried away by submarine.

George McGrath's article in the Police Gazette for December, 1960, entitled, "Positive Proof Hitler in Argentina" would bear out Nostradamus:

> Six weeks after Germany collapsed, a number of Nazi submarines sought refuge in the Argentine. The Argentine government acknowledged that some had arrived. But the most significant arrivals were kept secret.

> Allied intelligence knows that in the summer of 1945 Hitler and Eva Braun disembarked from a U-boat off the Argentine coast in the vicinity of San Clemente del Tuya. Eva was wearing masculine attire. One source of this information is a top Nazi who had also been landed by submarine. This man, nabbed long afterwards in Montevideo, Uruguay, received immunity from prosecution when he turned informer.

> Spruille Braden, then U. S. Ambassador to Argentina, received the San Clemente del Tuya report and asked the Argentine government for an explanation. Argentine officials insisted the report was false, but refused to give any further information. Braden thereupon sent U. S. intelligence operatives into the San Clemente del Tuya area.

> Shortly after Braden started his investigation, a respected democratic newspaper, *Critica*, published in Buenos Aires, reported from an authoritative government source that Hitler and his top Nazi aides had been transported to South America. The publisher immediately received this threat:

> "Stop the presses and suppress that story."

> *Critica* did not yield. A band of armed Nazis, shouting "Heil Hitler" and "Long Live Germany," stormed the paper and tried to burn down its building. Truckloads of newspapers were burned in the streets. Before the siege ended, two persons had been killed ...

> Braden has told the *Police Gazette:*

> "If the Argentine government had cooperated with us we could have captured the top Nazis. We had information from the best informed and most authoritative sources that

Hitler as well as Martin Bormann was hiding out in Patagonia.

"When I sent my agents there to investigate, they were ordered out of the region by armed guards who were Germans. Without the cooperation of the Argentine government, we were powerless to capture anyone there."

II
PROPHECIES OF DATED EVENTS

TWO DATES IN ONE PROPHECY

Around the year five hundred & eighty,*
One will await a very strange period;
In the year seven hundred & three (heavens to witness)
Many kingdoms one to five will make change.

En l'an cinq cens octante plus & moins,
On attend le siecle bien estrange;
En l'an sept cens & trois (cieux en tesmoins)
Que plusieurs regnes un a cinq feront change. (6.2)

THERE was a logical reason for the French seer placing the two
dates he did in the present prophecy. In both periods the nation was
concerned with wars of succession. "Around the year five hundred &
eighty" Henry III, King since 1574, was having his hands full with
rebellion. Historian Ferdinand Schevill writes, "A new element of
interest was introduced into the struggle only when it became clear
that Henry, who was the last male survivor of the reigning Valois
line, would leave no offspring. This opened the question of the succession." It was "a very strange period" indeed, for in it occurred the

* The *mil* (thousand) is understood, just as we are understood when we
leave out the thousands and hundreds and say simply, "the thirties, the forties,
the gay nineties," etc.

47

three-cornered War of the Three Henries (so it is known to history) involving

1. The protestant leader *Henry* of Navarre, opposed to King *Henry* and to *Henry* of Guise, leader of the ultra-Catholics.

2. *Henry* of Guise, opposed to the Protestant *Henry* and to King *Henry*,

3. *Henry* III, able to please neither and so forced to fight both.

The Huguenots had set up a self-governing republic "practically independent of the kingdom," and the right-wing Catholics had done the same with their Holy League.

In 1703 the War of the Spanish Succession is under way. Many nations were involved in this war. "It was literally universal and raged, at one and the same time, at all the exposed points of the French-Spanish possessions, that is, in the Spanish Netherlands, along the upper Rhine, in Italy, in Spain itself . . . on the sea, and in the colonies of North America." (Schevill)

The war began with the death of the King of Spain. When Louis XIV learned, to his great joy, that the throne had been left to his grandson, Philip, Duke of Anjou, he forgot his obligations to the British King William and sent the heir to Madrid (1702). William thereupon revived his Grand Alliance, a reconstituted coalition of the previous war, and attacked France. By 1703 five powers were involved against Louis: England, Austria, Holland, Germany and Portugal.

Prophecy Found in a Footnote

Anatole Le Pelletier's valuable reprint (1867) of the complete text of Nostradamus contains an important dated prophecy overlooked by Nostradamians because it is found only in a footnote. Now how could it be, the reader may ask, that lines of Nostradamus should be found only in such an obscure place? The story is interesting. In 1566, the year the prophet died, there appeared *A Lyon, chez Pierre Rigaud*, the first full text or *Editio Princeps* of the *Prophéties*. Two years later the Lyon edition reappeared in more perfect shape, with corrections and other alterations written in by the prophet himself just before his death. Now, in his 1867 reprint of the original 1566 text Le Pelletier includes in footnotes all the changes made by Nostradamus for the 1568 edition.

One of these changes occurs in the 1580 - 1703 quatrain already interpreted in the present book. Nostradamus, in re-reading his prophecy, decided to substitute for its last two lines two others containing an altogether new prediction. The two new lines read:

In the year seven hundred and nine heavens will be witness
That one will hardly be able to exchange gold for wheat.

En l'an sept cens et neuf cieux seront tesmoings,
Que pour de l'or en Bled non sans peine il change.

The prophecy is so clear and pointed it needs no other comment than direct quotations from the historians themselves:

1. Then came the terrible winter of 1708-9, such a winter as had never been known in the history of the country. Even the olive-trees in the south were killed by the severity of the cold. The king's servants begged in the street of Paris, and Madame de Maintenon and the dainty nobles of the court were glad to get even black bread to eat. Louis was in such need of money that he sold a service of gold plate to raise a few hundred thousand francs. (David *Montgomery, The Leading Facts of French History.*)

2. The spring of 1709 brought in a spell of bitter cold following on a mild winter, and the year's harvest was ruined. Corn was scanty and meat was unobtainable — the cattle had been slaughtered long before. The peasantry slaved in the fields, money was never seen; the whole French civilization seemed to be breaking down into a condition like that of the Stone Age. (C. S. Forester, *Louis XIV.*)

3. The fields were barren, the store-houses exhausted, the merchant ships were captured by the enemy, and the army, humiliated by frequent defeats, was perishing with hunger. The people became desperate. The king was ignominiously lampooned and placarded. He dared not appear in public, for starving crowds gathered around his carriage clamoring for bread. (Jacob Abbott, *History of Louis XIV.*)

4. The year of lowest vitality, the year of despair, was 1709. Louis in 1709 was ready to offer almost any terms for peace, (Hilaire Belloc, *Monarchy.*)

1607—ASTROLOGERS PERSECUTED

The number of astronomers will grow so great
Driven out, banished and books censured,
The year thousand six hundred and seven by sacred assemblies
That none will feel assured from the religious.

Croistra le nombres si grand des astronomes
Chassez, bannis et livres censurez,
L'an mil six cens et sept par sacrees glomes,
Que nul aux sacres ne seront asseurez. (8.71)

LAVER COMMENTS: "THE CURIOUS FACT IS THAT ASTROLOGY WAS CON-
demned in strong terms by the Council of Malines and that this
took place in 1607!" (When Nostradamus wrote, the distinction between astronomers and astrologers was hardly imagined. The astronomers of the time cast horoscopes.)

1660—INHERITOR OF THE TOADS

When the fork is held up by two pales,
With six half-horns and six open scissors,
The very powerful Lord, inheritor of the toads,
Will then put the whole world under him.

Quand le fourchu sera soustenu de deux paux,
Avec six demy-cors et six sizeaux ouverts,
Le tres puissant Seigneur, heritier des crapaux,
Alors subjugera sous soy tout l'univers.

THE TWO FIRST LINES DATE THIS QUATRAIN, WHICH WAS FIRST PUBLISHED
in 1605, 39 years after Nostradamus' death. The date so tortuosly told —
and yet in a manner so characteristic of an earlier age — is 1660.
The fork upheld by two pales or posts is the Roman M, the half-horn

the Roman C and the open scissors the Roman X. The total is MCCCCCCXXXXXX, or 1660.

This is a hit to within two months and nine days, for upon the death of Cardinal Mazarin on March 9, 1661, Louis XIV, France's glorious Sun-King, became the rightful inheritor of the toads of his Merovingian ancestors.

The subjects of Louis would not have considered the prophetic lines unusually flattering or fulsome. As a believer in the divine right of Kings, Nostradamus simply felt and described in advance what the baskers in the Sun themselves believed in all sincerity. Bossuet, the eloquent court preacher, with his monarch in mind, said, "Kings are gods; they bear on their forehead a divine character." Racine wrote, "The world, in seeing him, had recognized its master." The paintings on the walls of his Versailles showed Louis surrounded by gods and dis-comfited enemies, and by an ingenious method the sky at night held his name written in fire. "If constant adulation could have killed the king," says Montgomery, "he would have died young, for poets, preachers, orators, and historians vied with the nobles and with each other in praising his magnaminity, his glory, and his power. In Paris, bronze and marble statues and portraits of him abounded, and after every great victory some new monument or triumphal arch would be erected to do him honor."

> The moment Louis ascended to the throne to really rule he knew, with infallible instinct, the power he possessed. "On the news of the cardinal's death, the secretary of state obtained an audience with the king, then twenty-three. 'To whom, Sire,' he asked, 'shall we now apply for instructions?' 'To me,' replied Louis. The secretary was astonished, as well he might be, at the idea of the king's taking the management of the government directly into his own hands. But he found, with others, that the will of this young man was destined to be 'one of the strongest human elements in the seventeenth cen-tury.' Louis pursued the new policy not only with respect to the affairs of France, but also with the colonies, and the governor of Canada received orders to make his official reports directly to the crown. (Montgomery)

Writes his biographer Bartz: "He had succeeded in reducing to impotence all who might oppose his royal will — Parlement, the cities, the provincial diets, the nobility, the army, and all the institutions that had still ventured to make their voices heard in his father's day. Every

influence, every utterance in France was now in accord with the will
of the King, no one dared to contradict him. He was the supreme
overlord, the great autocrat whose word was final."

The Sun-King gave France the world's finest army, and through
Vauban's chain of forts the country was protected by an "Iron Frontier."
The monarch aspired to the conquest of Europe and proposed estab-
lishing a mighty empire in America. He achieved Louisiana, named
after him by the explorer La Salle.

More important, France conquered the mind of man. A host of great
writers made up some of the rays of the Sun-King. They included Corn-
eille, Racine, Moliere, Boileau, La Fontaine, La Bruyere, Fenelon,
Rochefoucauld, Madame de Sevigne, Descartes, Malebranche, and Pascal
— and throughout Europe these writers were read not in translation but
in the original French. Through their "Protector of Letters," this
wonderful language was also king, for it has remained the language of
diplomacy from that day to this.

FIRE OF LONDON IN "TWENTY-THREE THE SIXES"

The blood of the just will make complaint to London,
Burnt by fireballs in twenty-three the sixes;
The antique dame will fall from the high place,
Of the same sect many will be destroyed.

Le sang du juste à Londres fera faute,
Brulez par foudres de vingt trois les six;
La dame antique cherra de place haute,
De mesme secte plusieurs seront occis. (2.51)

NOSTRADAMIANS HAIL THIS PROPHECY AS A SUPER-TRIUMPH OF THE SEER.
It is a little under that: Nostradamus does not give the precise date for
the fire of London. "Twenty-three the sixes" is not 1666, no matter
how one juggles the figures. On the other hand the prophet comes remarkably close to the date by mention of "the sixes." Could he have

thought the fire took place on the twenty-third of the month? However, to predict the fire itself and set it in the sixes is no mean achievement.

St. Paul's Church, whose site was an ancient temple of Diana, was destroyed by the fire, as were eighty-seven other churches of the same denomination.

Nostradamus intimates that the fire of London was a punishment for the nation's crime of killing its king a few years earlier.

1700—TWO RELATED QUATRAINS

Twenty years after the reign of the moon passed,
Seven thousand years other will hold his monarchy,
When the sun takes his weary days,
Then is my Prophecy accomplished and ended.

Much, very much before these happenings,
Those of the East by virtue of the Moon,
The Year thousand seven hundred will make great depredations,
Subjugating almost the corner of Aquilon.

Vingt ans du regne de la lune passez,
Sept mils ans autre tiendra sa monarchie,
Quand le soleil prendra ses jours lassez,
Lors accomplit a fine ma Prophecie. (1.48)

Beaucoup, beaucoup avant telles menees,
Ceux d'Orient par la vertu Lunaire,
L'An mil sept cens feront grands emmenees,
Subjugant presque le coin Aquilonaire. (1.49)

THE TWO PROPHECIES ARE HERE QUOTED TOGETHER BECAUSE THE prophet obviously intended them to be read and understood together. The quatrains of Nostradamus do not follow chronologically the sequence in which they are published, but sometimes there are found clusters of two or three, as sequential cards are found in an imperfectly shuffled deck.

There shall be no more moon. What replaces him? Possibly a man-made satellite. Or possibly a planetoid, chained by earthlings to the orbit of earth.

The second quatrain of the "1700" prophecy is remarkable enough, for it was fulfilled on schedule, but in it Nostradamus seems to have put the cart before the horse.

To begin with, Aquilon (Boreas), the North Wind, a word used several times by the prophet, means in the quatrains *the land of the North Wind,* or *Russia. Coin Aquilonnaire* then signifies "corner of Russia," or "corner of the Land of the Far North." This corner was pretty well conquered by the warlike Charles XII of Sweden in November of the year 1700. Peter the Great of Russia, needing an outlet to the sea, had formed a Baltic alliance against Sweden, consisting of his Aquilon, Poland and Denmark. Charles decided that the best way to fight this formidable combination was to pick his enemies off one by one. His blitz crossing of the Baltic caught Denmark off guard, and the country collapsed. Next the eighteen year old conqueror tackled the Bear, the main body of whose forces were in Finland. When a bitter blizzard arose Charles cried exultantly, "Now with the storm at our backs they will never see how few we are!" Though tremendously outnumbered, his victory was devastating. The Russians were driven back with great slaughter. A bridge gave way beneath the throng of fugitives, states biographer of Charles, the Honorable Eveline Godley, and hundreds were drowned or crushed. "The whole Russian army — horse, foot and artillery, with all stores, ammunition and equipment — was in the hands of the conqueror." The victor was magnanimous. Except for the officers, whom he detained, he let the mighty army make its way back to the frontier.

Now the Swedish warlord was free to turn his attention to the remaining member of the Alliance. He defeated Augustus, the Saxon king of Poland, which gave the entire country to him, and through his influence Stanislaus Leczinsky was appointed king. Later, though, when Charles became the pursued instead of the pursuer, he took refuge in Turkey, where he was welcomed with great eclat as a superman. At the fortress of Bender, where he was given residence, he was received with every honor by the Turkish officials. "Before long, his ascendency in Turkish dominions seemed scarcely less than that of the Sultan himself." Through his native eloquence he managed to get two pro-Russian Grand Viziers overthrown and to persuade the Sultan to join forces with him in the conquest of Russia. A great victory over Peter the Great was achieved, but after this Charles' decline set in.

Now back to the prophecy. We are told that the corner of Aquilon will be conquered "by virtue of the moon." The original conquest by Charles in the year 1700 was done without Turkish help, but that help was called in at a later date, and during the course of the same war. * So Nostradamus, we see, gets the year right, and the place conquered, yet puts the cart before the horse.

"THE YEAR 1727, IN OCTOBER"

THE NEAR EAST CONQUEST

The third climate comprehended under Aries,
The year thousand seven hundred twenty & seven in October,
The King of Persia taken by those of Egypt,
Conflict, death, loss, great opprobrium to the cross.

*Le tiers climat sous Aries comprins,
L'ans mil sept cens vingt & sept en Octobre,
Le Roy de Perse par ceux d'Egypte prins,
Conflict, mort, perte, a la croix grand opprobre.* (3.77)

TURN TO DREYSS' Chronologie Universelle FOR THE FULFILLMENT OF this event.

Year 1727. Persia and Turkey. Treaty of peace (Oct.); the Turks keep all the country from Erivan, in Georgia, to Tauris and Hamadon; the Sultan of Constantinople is recognized as the legitimate successor of the caliphs.

Note that in the prophecy Nostradamus does not say "the Egyptians," but "those of Egypt," the distinction being the simple one made between the people of a country and its rulers. In 1727, those of Egypt were the Turks, who were Mohammedans, and the extension of whose power was therefore opprobrious to Christianity.

---

* "In 1700 Peter the Great entered upon a war with Sweden, which lasted till 1721." (Universal World Reference Encyclopaedia.)

The King of Persia was not kidnapped from the battle-field, but nevertheless he was truly "taken," or conquered. One sceptic, to whom I showed this quatrain, objected that the 1727, October treaty was not disadvantageous to the King of Persia; but the historians speak otherwise. According to A. L. Castellan, "The peace was very advantageous for the Turks, since they conserved proprietor-ship over a great part of this vast kingdom, and acknowledged superiority over almost all the rest." Sir John Malcolm writes, 'The provinces which the Turkish government possessed were granted in perpetuity. This included the whole of Kurdistan and Khuzistan, a part of Aderbijan and several cities in Irak." P. M. Sykes writes, "The provinces held by Turkey were ceded to the Sultan. In other words, Persia was dismembered."

When working on my first book on Nostradamus, out of curiosity I took this quatrain to a professor of mathematics at Columbia University, requesting him to calculate the odds against its fulfillment being merely a lucky hit. Here are his calculations:

Odds Against a Random Stroke

As the *Centuries* (meaning hundred verse sets) extend from the year 1555 to the year 3797 Nostradamus had — if no judgment were involved —

(1) One chance in 2242 (*i.e.*, 3797-1555) of guessing the right year.

(2) One chance in 12 of guessing the right month.

(3) One chance in $\dfrac{n(n-1)}{2}$ of guessing the right nations,

n standing for the number of nations in existence at the time the prophecy is due to be fulfilled. If there were 15 nations in existence at this time — actually there were many more — there would be 105 ways of selecting two of them.

(4) One chance in two of picking the victor.

(5) One chance in two of correctly stating the effect on the cross of the outcome of the war. In this case it is "great opprobrium." (Could be *for* or *against* the cross.)

Total possible chance of a random stroke is one in 2242 x 12 x 105 x 2 x 2 or 11,299,680.

Actually, for obvious reasons, the odds are much greater.

1792—RENOVATION OF THE CENTURY

NEXT I SHOWED THE PROFESSOR THE FOLLOWING PASSAGE FROM
Nostradamus' Dedicatory Epistle to Henry the Second:

> . . . then will come the beginning including in itself what
> will endure, and starting that same year there will be the
> greatest persecution of the Christian Church, worse than that
> which took place in Africa, and this will culminate in the
> year 1792 which people will think to be a renovation of the age.

> . . . et comencant icelle annee sera faicte plus grande persecu-
> tion a l'Eglise Chestienne que n'a este faicte en Afrique, et
> durera ceste-icy jusques a l'an mil sept cens nonante deux, que
> l'on cuydera estre une renovation de siecle.

A new era is a renovation of the age, and France's new era — one
of the most important and fateful in all history — was the royalty-
uprooting Revolution. Now 1792, the date given by Nostradamus, brings
us right into the thick of the Revolution. More: the prophet associates
this year and this new era with a terrible persecution of the Christian
Church. When Nostradamus wrote, the Church was securely established in France. The country was Catholic: it still is. Yet the year
1792 brings us into the midst of a frightful persecution of the clergy,
with few precedents in history, and with none in France. More: so
much did the Reds of the Revolution hate Christianity that they abolished
the "Anno Domini" Calendar, and proclaimed Year One of the
Republic. When? Specifically, on September 21, 1792. Not a year
earlier, not a year later.*

"They will *think* it to be a renovation of time," writes the prophet.
Surely! Did not this anti-Christian new era foolishness officially end

---

* Carlyle makes merry in his sardonic way with the New Calendar. In his
French Revolution he writes:

Marechal the Atheist, almost ten years ago, proposed a New Calendar, free
at least from superstition: this the Paris Municipality would now adopt, in defect
of a better; at all events, let us have either this of Marechal's or a better, — the
New Era being come. Petitions, more than once, have been sent to that effect; and
indeed, for a year past, all Public Bodies, Journalists, and Patriots in general, have
dated *First Year of the Republic*. It is a subject not without difficulties. But the
Convention has taken it up . . .

Four equal Seasons, Twelve equal Months of Thirty days each; this makes
three hundred and sixty days: and five odd days remain to be disposed of. The

on January 1, 1806, and the French return to the Christian Calendar, which they still use?

Nostradamus has associated these facts exactly as the historians have done. When they write of the persecution of the Church they discuss at the same time Year One of the Republic, mentioning that this new era began in 1792, and that it was a direct result of the anti-Christian program of the Republicans.

"What are the odds here?" I asked the Professor.

"2242, since the month is not given, but just the year."

"But," I said, "Nostradamus has correctly associated *two* facts with this year, not one. That must increase the odds greatly."

"Actually the odds are incalculable," he replied.

But keeping these odds on a conservative and calculable basis (absurdly low), the chances of the prophet accidentally hitting off both these dated predictions is one in 11,299,680 x 2242 or 25,311,-283,200.

And these are not the only prophecies to which Nostradamus has affixed the correct dates!

(As to the undated prophecies, their analysis must be qualitative rather than quantitative; yet an approximation to a quantitative analysis may be made of even some of these.)

---

five odd days we will make Festivals, and name the five Sansculottides, or Days without Breeches . . .

Vernal Equinox, at midnight for the meridian of Paris, in the year whilom Christian 1792, from that moment shall the New Era reckon itself to begin. *Vendemiaire, Brumaire, Frimaire;* or as one might say, in mixed English, *Vintagearious, Fogarious, Frostarious*: these are our three Autumn months. *Nivose, Pluviose, Ventose,* or say, *Snowous, Rainous, Windous,* make our Winter season. *Germinal, Floreal, Prairial,* or *Buddal, Floweral, Meadowal,* are our Spring season. *Messidor, Thermidor, Fructidor,* that is to say (*dor* being Greek for *gift*) *Reapidor, Heatidor, Fruitidor,* are Republican Summer . . There are three Decades, then, in each of the months; which is very regular; and the *Decadi,* or Tenth-day, shall always be the "Day of Rest." And the Christian Sabbath, in the case? Shall shift for itself!

18th OF BRUMAIRE

NAPOLEON'S COUP D'ETAT

By Mars contrary the Monarchy
Of the great fisherman will be in ruinous trouble;
Young red king will take the hierarchy,
The brigands will go out on a day of fog.

Par Mars contraire sera la Monarchie
Du grand pescheur en trouble ruyneux;
Jeune noir rouge prendra la hierarchie,
Les prodifeurs iront jour bruyneux. (6.25)

THE YOUNG RED KING WAS NAPOLEON, KNOWN TO THE FRENCH AS
"child of the Revolution." ("Young red king," not "young red black."
Nostradamus uses *noir* seventeen times as an anagram of king.) During
his early campaigns, in 1796-1797, "he began a new and disgraceful
system of pillage. He stripped the Vatican at Rome and the churches,
libraries, and picture galleries of the conquered country, of their
choicest treasures, carrying paintings, statuary, books, and manuscripts
to Paris to enrich the palace of the Louvre with stolen splendor. Thus
Italy was for the first time robbed of her great works of art by one
who was himself an Italian." (Montgomery)

When young Buonaparte returned from Egypt in 1799, he learned
that the five-man Directory had plundered the Vatican of more of its
treasures, and had ended by carrying the Pope to France, where he
died this same year.

Having the confidence of the people, Napoleon put himself at the
head of affairs and deliberately overthrew the Directory. The day of
the coup d'etat, November 9, 1799, is known to history by its Republican revolutionary name, *The Eighteenth of Brumaire. Brumaire*
means "day of fog."

13th OF FEBRUARY

ASSASSINATION OF DUC DE BERRI

Head of Fossano will have his throat cut
By the keeper of the hounds and greyhounds:
The deed perpetrated by those of the Tarpeian rock,
Saturn in Leo 13 of February.

Chef de Fossan aura gorge couppee
Par le ducteur du limier et levrier;
Le faict patre par ceux du mont Tarpee,
Saturne en Leo 13 de Fevrier. (3.96)

THE DUC DE BERRI, THROUGH HIS MOTHER, MARIE-THERESE OF SAVOY,
was a Prince of Sardinia and therefore a head or chief of Fossano.
The town boasts an impressive ducal palace which was frequented by
the royalty and nobility of Sardinia, — and France. Fossano was the
equivalent of the British Windsor. Nostradamus was interested in a
"head of Fossano," who, as son to the future Charles X was heir
to the throne of France.

On the evening of February 13th, the Duc de Berry left the opera
early because his wife was indisposed. As he was helping her into the
carriage, a man rushed up to him and plunged a knife into his body.
The victim fell with the cry, "I am dead. I am holding the hilt of the
dagger."

His assassin was the brooding anti-royalist Louvel, satisfied to
kill any legitimate heir to the throne of France. Nostradamus was in
error. Louvel was not "the keeper of the hounds and greyhounds."
He was a saddler. But one of his jobs was to manufacture leashes, —
by which hounds and greyhounds are led about. And he was in the
royal pay, as the prophecy implies.

"Will have his throat cut" is a locution for "be assassinated." A
man may be called a cut-throat even if he slays by some other means
than slitting wind-pipes.

The crime aroused horror throughout France and among all parties.
The Paris Opera House was razed as an accursed spot. "A vast conspiracy was believed to exist . . . The liberals thought they were ruined,
because a reaction seemed inevitable." "Nobody would believe that

the crime was an isolated crime." (Imbert de St. Amand) But Louvel insisted he was a lone wolf: "They want to make me commit a second crime by trying to force me to name my accomplices, when I have none." Nevertheless, President Seguier was right, "There exists a permanent conspiracy against the Bourbons." The anti-royalist press and pamphlets of the day were vicious and Louvel had devoured them until the poison bore its fruit.

As Nostradamus says, the deed was "perpetrated by those of the Tarpeian rock." The image is borrowed from the revolutionists themselves. No doubt it grew out of that other symbol of violence, "the Mountain." Marat's speeches refer to the Tarpeian rock, from which enemies of the Republic were hurled to their death, and Kropotkin, in his *History of the French Revolution,* picks up the vivid image from the journals and speeches of that bloody time.

To return to the second line of the prophecy: "By the keeper of the hounds and greyhounds." This near-hit is remarkable enough. Louvel had followed the Duc de Berri to the chase for four years. And one time, relates the Comte d'Artois, the young man's father:

> The Duke of Berry, returning from the chase, and slowly ascending the mountain in the forest of Fontainebleau, noticed a man who seemed fatigued. The prince summoned his huntsman, told him to take the man up behind the carriage and ask him if he were suffering and what was his name. "He is not sick," answered the huntsman, "he is only tired. His name is Louvel, and he works in the king's stables at Versailles, where he lives with his sister." On reaching the summit of the mountain, Louvel got down from the carriage, and no more was thought about him.

It is possible that Nostradamus, scrying the future fates of his kings and their offspring, picked up this picture.

"THREE AND SEVENTY"

DEATH OF NAPOLEON III

The driven from the reign will return,
Her enemies found conspirators;
More than ever her time will triumph,
Three and seventy, death, too assured.

La dechassee au regne tournera,
Ses ennemis trouvez des conjurez;
Plusque jamais son temps triomphera,
Trois et septante, la mort, trop asseurez. (6.74)

THE NOSTRADAMIANS HAVE TUSSLED WITH THIS QUATRAIN TO LITTLE avail. Yet its correct application does not seem difficult. The Empire, driven out with Napoleon I, was restored under Napoleon III, and "more than ever" its time triumphed. The Corsican had to wage war constantly to maintain his Empire, while his nephew had relatively long periods of peace in which to do some really wonderful things for France. "Where there had been mazes of narrow, crooked, and filthy streets, he laid out magnificent boulevards, straight as an arrow . . . At the same time he built a system of sewers superior to that of any capital in Europe or America . . . The most beautiful city in the world had now become more beautiful than ever." (Montgomery) In 1869 he completed the Suez Canal.

Guerard, biographer of Napoleon III, writes:

On more practical ground than prestige, France in 1867 had enjoyed fifteen years of order and prosperity. Not without shadows and misgivings, to be sure. But the wealth of the country was no dream, and no permanent loss of momentum was perceptible. The economy of France was still dynamic . . . The reconstruction of Paris, the most sensational achievement of the Empire, was in its main lines completed. The great Exposition, admirably planned by the Catholic sociologist Le Play, was immensely larger and more brilliant than that of 1855. It revealed the industrial development of the age; and in quality if not in bulk, France could hold her own against England or Germany. Princess, kings, emperors, entertained three and five at a time, seemed to pay court to their overlord. Never had the glamour of Parisian life enjoyed such a universal appeal. Aristocrats, wits, and *philosophes* flocked to the eighteenth-century *salons* in their hundreds; but now farmers and merchants, athirst for a more brilliant and freer life, came in their myriads from the ends of the world.

The Franco-Prussian war ended the glory and glamour with most assured certainty. France was ignominiously defeated, the Emperor captured, and soon he fled as an exile to England, there to die under the surgeon's knife, in the year eighteen *seventy-three.*

III

PROPHECIES OF PERIODS OF TIME

"BEFORE EIGHTEEN"

THE DEATH OF FRANCIS II

First son of widow, unfortunate marriage
With no children, two Isles in discord,
Before eighteen, incompetent age.
The accord of the other will be still earlier.

Premier fils vefve malheureux mariage
Sans nuls enfants, deux Isles en discord,
Avant dix-huict incompetant age.
De l'autre pres plus bas sera l'accord. (10.39)

THE sickly Francis II, eldest son of Catherine de Medici, widow of Henri II, came to the throne in his 16th year and "ruled" France for about 17 months, dying December 15, 1560, without children. Since he had been born January 19, 1543, "before eighteen" is a precise statement: he lived to be a month and a half short of eighteen years.

Upon his death his beautiful widow, Mary Stuart, packed up and left for Scotland. The discord her visitation brought the British Isles is too well-known to need rehearsal here.

With the death of Francis his ten year old brother Charles IX ascended the throne. The following year he was affianced to Elizabeth of Austria.

This prophecy was famous before fulfilled. Michieli, Venetian Ambassador to the Court of France, wrote: "Each courtier remembers the thirty-ninth quatrain of Centurie X of Nostradamus and comments upon it under his breath." Again, he wrote, "There is another prediction very widespread in France emanating from the famous astrologer called Nostradamus and which menaces the three brothers, saying that the Queen will see them all kings."

"SHE WILL WEEP FOR GRIEF SEVEN YEARS"

JULY, 1559 — AUGUST 1, 1566

The Queen alone left to the reign,
Her unique extinguished first on the field of honor;
She will weep for grief seven years,
Then long life to the reign by great fortune.

La Dame seule au regne demeuree,
D'unic esteint premier au lict d'honneur;
Sept ans sera de douleur esploree,
Puis longue vie au regne par grand heur. (6.63)

CATHERINE DE MEDICI, NOSTRADAMUS' BELOVED PATRONESS, NEVER GOT over the tragedy of the tournament that made her a widow. She said, "It is a wound which brought to me principally and to all the kingdom so much evil that I cannot think on that day I can do anything good." Left alone to the reign, she wrote sadly soon after to her daughter, the Queen of Spain: "God has left me with three small children and a wholly divided kingdom." Not until August 1, 1566 did she put off her widow's weeds, having worn them for seven years and a few days. She lived for another twenty-three years.

J. W. Thompson, in *The Wars of Religion in France,* writes of her qualifications as a ruler: "The power was all in Catherine's hand . . . France began to awaken to the fact that the queen who had led a life of retirement during her husband's reign, in that of her son was evincing that capacity for public affairs which was an hereditary possession in her family . . . She governed as if she were king. She appointed to offices and to benefices; she granted pardon; she kept the seal; she had the last word to say in council; she opened the letters of the ambassador and other ministers. Those who used to think she was a timid woman discovered that her courage was great."

Catherine de Medici
"She kept the seal; she had the last word to say in council."

"SEVEN YEARS AFTER WILL BE OF CONTRARY PARTY"

The great pilot will be appointed by the King,
Will leave the fleet to attain higher place:
Seven years after will be of contrary party,
Barbaran army will come to fear Venice.

Le grand pillot par Roy sera mande,
Laisser la classe pour plus haut lieu atteindre:
Sept ans apres sera contrebande,
Barbare armee viendra Venise craindre. (6.75)

GASPAR DE COLIGNY, APPOINTED GRAND-ADMIRAL BY HENRY II IN 1552, gave up his post in 1559, on the death of the King, to become head of the Huguenots. Seven years later, in 1567, he headed their rebellion in the civil war. He was assassinated in 1572, during the St. Bartholomew massacre. In 1571 the Venetians gained the victory of Lepanto over the Turks, one of the most celebrated naval battles in history.

"OF SEVEN MONTHS"

ATTACK ON CADIZ

Before the lake where rich treasure was cast
Of seven months, and its host discomfited
The Spaniards will be plundered by the Albions,
By delay loss in giving the conflict.

Devant le lac ou plus cher fut gette
De sept mois, et son ost desconfit
Seront Hispans par Albanois gastez,
Par delay perte en donnant le conflict. (8.94)

IN JUNE, 1596, ESSEX, HOWARD AND RALEIGH MADE A DEVASTATING attack on Cadiz Bay, where many Spanish galleons, with rich treasure, lay stranded in the harbor, after a seven month voyage from South

America. The English raiders destroyed thirteen ships of war and forty of the galleons. Ward says,

> Had the Spaniards been alert, they might have unloaded the treasure-ships, and so saved the cargoes. If they had attacked the English at once, instead of awaiting the onset, they might have beaten them off, or at least have kept them out of the harbour. But they were so supine that the Duke de Medina had at last to fire the ships to prevent their capture . . .
>
> The bay and harbour of Cadiz may very well be called a lake, being twelve miles one way, and at least six the other, whilst the entrance to it from Rota to the Castle of St. Sebastian is a good six miles. When Essex got possession of the Castle of Puntales, he commanded the whole town and harbour. The idea of *lake* is actually expressed in the very name of Cadiz, which is derived from the Punic word *Gaddir*, an *enclosed place*.

"SEVEN AND FIFTY PACIFIC YEARS"

1657 - 1715

> The walls will be reduced from brick to marble,
> Seven & fifty pacific years,
> Joy to humans, the aqueduct renewed,
> Health, great fruits, joy & mellifluous time.

> *De brique en marbre seront les murs reduicts,*
> *Sept & cinquante annees pacifique,*
> *Joye aux humains, renove l'aqueduct,*
> *Sante, grands fruits, joye & temps melifique.* (10.89)

THE BATTLE OF THE DUNES WAS WON BY LOUIS XIV'S FORCES UNDER Turenne in 1657, and "this was the end," as Bainville states. "Peace now reigned at home." (Montgomery) Louis was not the most peaceful monarch in the world but he managed to keep his wars outside of France instead of in it. As he boasted to de Villars: "Since there must be war, it is better to wage it against my enemies than against my children." He held to this ideal till the day of his death, September 1, 1715.

The fifty-seven years were peaceful, according to the historians. Jacques Bainville writes that Louis's reign "has one dominant characteristic: there was complete tranquillity within the realm . . . There was to be an end of those troubles, those civil wars whose incessant return had wrought such desolation. This prolonged calm and the absence of invasions bear witness to what a high degree of civilization and of wealth France had attained. Order within and security without; these are the ideal conditions of prosperity. Voltaire in his *Century* of Louis XIV, stated: 'All was peaceful during his reign.' "

In his reign, as Nostradamus predicted, the walls were "reduced from brick to marble." "He lived in a frenzy of building," says Bartz. "In his epoch," states Belloc, came "some of the greatest works in engineering and building . . . The splendour is apparent still in the domes and the palaces." Conceived by the King, Versailles, Marly and Trianon arose in glory. Versailles was the most gorgeous of the palaces. "Everything was of multi-colored marble" (Bartz.) The walls were *"reduced* from brick to marble." Stated the engineer Vauban: "If the old palace is pulled down, I shall build it up again stone by stone." "Hence," remarks Bartz, "it was necessary to make the old structure the centre of the new to the detriment of symmetry."

Canals were included in the building frenzy. The most important of these, and a canal ever after famous, was that of Midi, which joins the Atlantic and the Mediterranean. It was undertaken by Pierre Paul Riquet (1604-1680), who had charge of the system of water in the province of Languedoc. In 1662 he submitted his project to Colbert. The enthusiastic minister interested Louis XIV in it. But not till 1666 were difficulties vanquished and an edict issued, authorizing Riquet to commence his immense work. Because of insufficient funds, he consecrated his fortune to the project and went through fourteen years of unheard of labor. He died six months before the canal was completed. The aqueduct was "renewed," as Nostradamus predicted. After a lapse of years the work was completed by his son and formally taken over by the Intendant of Guyenne and Languedoc.

This extraordinary age was a mellifluous time indeed, about which more may be read in the comment on the 1660 quatrain on page 50.

"WHEN THE ROSE IS IN BLOOM"

DEATH OF PIUS VI

Roman Pontiff beware of approaching
The city watered by two rivers.
You will come to spit your blood near there,
Your and yours when the rose is in bloom.

Romains Pontife garde de t'approcher
De la cite que deux fleuves arrouse.
Ton sang viendra aupres de la cracher,
Toy et les tiens quand fleurira la rose. (2.97)

NOSTRADAMUS REFERS IN SEVERAL QUATRAINS TO THE SAD FATE OF PIUS the Sixth, in whom, says the Britannica, "the fortunes of the Papacy had reached perhaps their lowest point since the Middle Ages." In a prophecy descriptive of the Montgolfier balloon and naming its inventors, Nostradamus states, "The renown of Sext, the Cornerstone will fail," (See page 133) and in another quatrain clearly related to the same period (See page 26) the prophet remarks, "Great cornerstone will die three leagues from the Rhone." In the quatrain under present consideration Nostradamus gives further details.

Pius the Sixth and his family were stripped of all they possessed, as a result of orders given to the Army by the hard-hearted Directory and he was then unceremoniously brought to France, accompanied by thirty-two priests. Old and dying, he was taken to Valence, near Lyons, city watered by two rivers*, where he passed away two months later, on August 29, 1799.

The sorrows of his last days were a little alleviated by the beauty of his surroundings. He was kept prisoner next to "a garden in the form of a terrace where he was able to win back a little life." "The garden dominated the town and the course of the Rhone." (Franclieu, historian of Valence) "Oh, what a beautiful view," exclaimed the

---

* Speaking of the French Revolution, Nostradamus writes in another quatrain, "Le mal viendra au joinct de Saone & Rhosne." (See page 24)

Pontiff at first sight of the flourishing garden. Morelli, in *Archives de M. Mazimbert*, 1799, July, wrote gratefully, "His Holiness is breathing a good air, thanks to the wheel-chair promenades." The Municipal officers prepared a chapel for him in the middle of the garden, where he prayed and saw visitors.

He died, at the age of eighty-two, after "violent sufferings accompanied with expectorations and vomitings." (Franclieu)

KING OF SARDINIA FOR THREE YEARS

(DECEMBER, 1798 — JUNE, 1802)

In Sardinia a noble King will come,
Who will only hold the kingdom for three years.
Several colors will be conjoined to it,
As for him, he will sleep after care, afflicted and scorned.

Dans la Sardeigne un noble Roy viendra,
Qui tiendra que trois ans le royaume.
Plusieurs couleurs avec soy conjoindra,
Luy mesme apres soin sommeil marrit scome. (8.88)

THIS QUATRAIN HAS BEEN DEALT WITH MORE FULLY IN *"Nostradamus on Napoleon."* Suffice it here to say that Charles Emmanuel IV resigned his continental estates to the French tricolor in December, 1798, and fled to the Island of Sardinia, which he ruled till June, 1802, three and a half years. Then, says his biographer, Menabrea, "Broken . . . he went to die at Rome," though he had seventeen sad years more to live, in a Jesuit novitiate cell.

According to *Larousse*, the Kingdom of Sardinia was *created* in 1720, more than a hundred and fifty years after Nostradamus penned this prophecy concerning one of its kings.

FOURTEEN YEAR TYRANNY OF THE CROPHEAD

NOVEMBER 9, 1799 - APRIL 13, 1814

From the marine and tributary city
The crop-head will take the satrapy:
To drive out as sordid those who are contrary;
For fourteen years he will hold the tyranny.

De la cite marine et tributaire
La teste rase prendra la satrapie:
Chasser sordide qui puis sera contraire;
Par quatorze ans tiendra la tyrannie. (7.13)

THIS QUATRAIN, WITH TWO OTHERS ON THE "CROP-HEAD," IS INTERPRETED at length in volume two, *Nostradamus on Napoleon,* so here I shall only summarize the facts behind the prophecy. Napoleon, known to his soldiers as *le petit tondu,* "the little crop head," first found fame at the siege of Toulon, which he took from the English, who were holding it for the French royalists. He drove out as sordid the five members of the Directory, for "there had been much speculation, and some of it was coming to light." (H. G. Wells, *Outline of History.*) For fourteen years he held the tyranny.

SEVEN PROSPEROUS YEARS

1830 - 1838

Seven years Philip will have prosperous fortune:
He will put down the effort of the Arabs;
Then in his midday affair against the grain,
Young Ogmion will overwhelm his fort.

Sept ans sera Philipp fortune prospere:
Rabaissera des Arabes l'effort;

> *Puis son midy perplex rebors affaire,*
> *Jeune Ognion abismera son fort.* (9.89)

LOUIS-PHILIPPE RULED FRANCE FROM JULY, 1830 TO FEBRUARY, 1848.
His first seven years were prosperous. According to Maurois:

> Towards 1838, the regime's position seemed fairly strong;
> it had lasted, and that was a great merit. It was backed by the
> mass of the peasants, because it afforded them peace, pros-
> perity- and good roads. Guizot had bettered primary educa-
> tion, and Thiers had done as much for the public monuments.
> Lastly the Algerian war had added to the prestige of the King's
> sons, since they had fought in it with distinction . . . The con-
> quest of Algeria, begun during the last days of Charles X's
> reign, continued gloriously."

But in Louis-Philippe's midday things went much against the
grain. The Eastern situation rose up again, this time to disgrace him.
France was restless, and romantically avid for glory, which included
war.

> Universal suffrage would have saved the monarchy. A
> limited suffrage, which gave the vote to a disgruntled middle
> class bred on Voltaire, brought about its overthrow. The
> secret societies were rich. In the Chambers, in the streets, a
> mounting tide of rebellion rose against the younger branch of
> the royal house. There were riots at Lyon, at Grenoble, in
> Paris. At Strasbourg and Boulogne a nephew of the great
> Napoleon tried to seize power. A legitimist tide swept across
> La Vendee. To a grumbling mutter of plots and insurrections
> the reign of Louis-Philippe drew to a close. (Sedillot)

"Young Ogmion will overwhelm his fort," concludes the quatrain. *Ogmion* is Oignon, onion, the bulb of the Lily, the common
people, the Republic. *Ognion* is the Celtic Mercury, the Gallic Hercules.
Charles Ward writes: "It has figured in 1792, 1848, and again after
the German war, 1872. At the two first periods they put the figure of
this Hercules on their five franc pieces, with that idle exergue, Liberte,
Egalite, Fraternite." Elsewhere Nostradamus writes, "le grand mercure
d'Hercule fleur de lys." (10.79) The young Republic, weary of its
king, overwhelmed his bastion of Paris.

The prophecy not only names a King of France but numbers
his years of prosperity.

SEVENTEEN YEAR REIGN

AUGUST 9, 1830 - FEBRUARY 24, 1848

After the throne has been held seventeen years,
Five will change at the termination of that period:
Then one will be elected at the same time,
Who will not be too much conformed to the Romans.

Apres le siege tenu dix-sept ans,
Cinq changeront en tel revolu terme:
Puis sera l'un esleu de mesme temps,
Qui des Romains ne sera trop conforme. (5.92)

SINCE NOSTRADAMUS' TIME ONLY ONE RULER OF FRANCE HELD THE throne for seventeen years: the avaricious monarch, Louis-Philippe, son of the treacherous Duke of Orleans. When revolution drove him from the throne, five others lost out. Says Maurois, "Louis-Philippe had five sons, all strong and handsome — Orleans, Nemours, Joinville, Aumale and Montpensier."

The ruler who followed was elected. Louis-Napoleon, nephew of the Emperor of glorious memory, was made President of France. The election of this rather complex personality was a sign for rejoicing in Rome. He had in the past supported the claims of Italian nationalism. And now that the Pope had fled Rome, the Austrians been driven out and under the influence of Garibaldi and Mazzini a republic been proclaimed, the Romans looked expectantly in the direction of France for support. "But what could Louis do? He did not deny — he never denied — his interest in the liberation of Italy: but he was pledged, as President, to a policy of peace. Charles Albert's cause was that of all Italians; but if France were his ally she would be fighting not merely against Austria, but against the Pope; and the President, whatever his private views about Papal misrule, could not so antagonize the clerical vote which had helped to put him in power." (J. M. Thompson) So, instead of supporting the new Roman republic he sent his troops to crush it and reinstate the Pope. This done, however, he drew back to his middle of the road policy.

Louis' policy was the same in both capitals: to stand as the champion of Order between the opposite extremes of reaction and revolution. But order, in his mind, and in the scheme of his Empire, included Law and Liberalism; it was for all parties in the state, poor as well as rich, anti-clerical as well as Catholics; yes, and for foreigners as well as Frenchmen. So, whilst the Catholics were still rubbing their hands over the occupation of Rome, he published a letter to his aide-de-camp Edgar Ney (whose name was itself a Napoleonic memory) declaring that 'the French republic had not sent an army to Rome to stifle Italian liberty', and that the help given to the Pope was conditional on his granting a general amnesty, adopting the *Code Napoleon*, and introducing a liberal administration. (Thompson)

To recapitulate on the fulfillment of this prophecy. The only ruler of France to occupy the throne for seventeen years was Louis-Philippe; he had five sons, who naturally could not succeed their father after a revolution which was followed by the advent of the new Napoleon; the successor to the ruler of seventeen years was, as Nostradamus predicted, "elected," and he was most certainly not too much conformed to the Romans. Note too that there was a vital Roman question precisely at the termination of the seventeen year period.

"SEVEN MONTH GREAT WAR"

JULY 19, 1870 — FEBRUARY 26, 1871

Fire from heaven on the Royal edifice,
When the light of Mars fails,
Seven month great War, dead malefic people,
Rouen Evreux, to the King will not fail.

De feu celeste au Royal edifice,
Quand la lumiere du Mars deffaillira,
Sept mois grand' Guerre, mort gent de malefice,
Rouen Evreux, au Roy ne faillira. (4.100)

MARS SIGNIFIES WAR, BUT IN SEVERAL QUATRAINS OF NOSTRADAMUS (to be discussed in a later volume) it also refers specifically to Napoleon III. Nostradamus seems not to have been too fond of the Emperor, hence the ironic dubbing. Louis Napoleon loudly proclaimed peace but was sometimes led to warlike acts. Historians differ. To some, he was a man of excellent good will; to others, of negative influence on his nation.

After the light of Mars failed and a provisional government was set up under Thiers, civil war broke out in the capital. The Paris Commune, believing the government had betrayed the country in making peace with Germany closed the gates of the city and "from that time for more than two months (March 18 to May 21, 1871), an armed force of two hundred thousand men had complete control of the metropolis." Socialists, Communists, Anarchists, Destructionists did their capital all the damage they could. They set fire to the palace of the Tuileries, the Hotel de Ville, the Palais Royal, the Courts of Justice, and many other public buildings. MacMahon's troops extinguished some of the conflagrations, but Versailles was reduced to blackened ruins. Were these wicked deeds among the *Chatiments?* Many thought the burning of the Tuileries part of "God's judgement made manifest through the people's holy wrath."

"Dead, malefic people," predicts Nostradamus. The insurgents made their last stand in the cemetery of Pere la Chaise and vicinity. "There, hundreds of men, women, and children were mowed down with bullets and grapeshot, and their mutilated bodies fell dead and dying among the shattered tombs. Thus for the time ended the Commune. It had destroyed property to the amount of five hundred million francs. The number of killed was estimated at twenty thousand." (Montgomery) Yet, they had been malefic people. With the capture of some of their leaders by the forces under Thiers, in reprisal the Commune had seized the venerable Archbishop Darboy, "a man whose life had been spent in deeds of charity among the poor, also the President of the Court of Cassation — 'the highest judicial dignitary in France' — and sixty-four priests, besides a number of other citizens." These were held as hostages, and later, deliberately massacred.

Rouen was occupied by the German troops. It did not fail the King (or Emperor) in loyalty, however. When Kaiser Wilhelm expressed his intention of stopping at the town to review the occupation troops, Mayor Neties replied "with magnificent insolence," "Your king is a soldier: I will give him a billet of lodging." Kaiser Wilhelm took the hint.

The town took on the aspect of national mourning. Black flags and drapes were everywhere, in the windows of stores, and on patriotic statues, including one of Joan of Arc. Skull and crossbone streamers were daringly set up at the military post of Lacroix Isle. The visiting Emperor of Brazil, Don Pedro de Bragance, in the town for a short stay, refused to contact the Prussian authorities.

Evreux, also occupied, may have behaved similarly. The newspapers of the time would probably enlighten us.

TWO HUNDRED AND NINETY YEARS

You will see the British nation change seven times.
Tainted in blood in two hundred and ninety years;
France not so, by reason of Germanic support;
Aries doubts her Bastarnan pole.*

*Sept fois changer verrez gent Britannique
Teints en sang en deux cens nonante an;
Franche non point, par appuy Germanique;
Aries doubte son pole Bastarnan.* (6.57)

BY *teints en sang* NOSTRADAMUS DOES NOT MEAN THAT ENGLAND IS to have a bloodier history than his native land. In fact the many prophecies of Nostradamus on the French civil wars and revolutions are enough to negate this thought. *Teints* is not *tasché* or *souillé*. The prophet simply means that the throes of change and revolution undergone by England will break up the continuity of her divine and royal line. No so in the land of the Franks. And oddly enough, despite the terrible turmoils France has so long suffered, the contrast is justified. David Montgomery, in his *Leading Facts of French History*, states: "From Hugh Capet descended every sovereign — the Napoleons only excepted — that has since ruled the country."

Nostradamus predicts for England seven changes of government in 290 years. Since this prophecy was penned and published shortly before Protestant Elizabeth succeeded Catholic Mary we will begin with 1558, the year of the Virgin Queen's accession. Two hundred and ninety years

---

* Poland (*la Bastarnie*) has been dismembered many times since the writing of the prophecy.

added to that brings us to 1848, a year most important for all Europe, including England. Many history books mark 1848 as a year of historical departure, a year in which the bourgeoisie began to come into its own. And as in France and the rest of the continent, so in England.

Indeed, Raymond Postgate, in his fascinating book, *Story of a Year 1848*, describing the culmination of the Chartist Movement in England, concludes: "It was the last attempt ever made at a revolution in Britain:" In itself, the Chartist attempt to give the people universal suffrage and other benefits was not a failure. The seeds it planted in its attention-getting attempt at revolution bore fruit in the years to come, as we all know.

The Chartist Movement even tried to imitate in a respectable way some of the aspects of the French Revolution of 1792. "Their eyes were on France: 'We'll respect the law, if the law-makers respect us; if they don't — France is a Republic" said Ernest Jones, their most intelligent leader. They seemed almost to think they *were* in France; their delegate meeting which met on April 4th was called 'The Convention', as if the year had been 1792 and the city Paris. Julian Harney, their most ferocious speaker, called himself the Friend of the People and by a careful, open-shirted disarray made himself look as much like Marat as he could without raising ridicule." (Postgate) And Louis Napoleon was a London constable, in case there should be trouble.

The terminal points predicted by Nostradamus for the important seven changes for the British people are then 1558 and 1848. Let us see if those changes add up to seven:

1. 1558 - 1603, Tudor Elizabeth.
2. Beginning of Stuart Dynasty, 1603-1649.
3. No king. Republic under Cromwell, 1649-1660.
4. Restoration of Stuarts, 1660-1685.
5. Stuarts driven out and House of Orange installed, 1685-1714.
6. House of Hanover takes English throne, 1714.
7. 1848. "It was the last attempt ever made at a revolution in Britain." (Postgate)

IV

PROPHECIES FULFILLED IN THE 16th AND 17th CENTURIES

THE MURDER AT BLOIS: PROPHECY ONE

In the year when a one-eyed man reigns in France
The Court will be in a very grievous trouble:
The Great One of Blois will kill his friend;
The kingdom put in evil and double doubt.

En l'an qu'un oeil en France regnera
La Cour sera en un bien fascheux trouble:
Le Grand de Blois son amy tuera;
Le regne mis en mal et doute double. (3.55)

EXACTLY as Nostradamus predicted, "in the year when a one-eyed man reigned "in France the Court was in a very grievous trouble." And it was in that same grievous trouble *because* the King was a one-eyed man. Henry II lived for about eleven days after his terrible accident, so the prophecy is as precise as one could wish: the one-eyed king reigned *in the year* . . . Sedillot writes, "With the death of Henry II everything fell apart. It needed no more than an ill-fated splinter of wood in the royal eye during the tournament to reveal how fragile was the Valois power." Bainville is in agreement: "The death of Henry II precipitated matters . . . His son, Francis II, was only sixteen years old and was, moreover, a sickly child. It was during his reign of one year, that the Catholics and Protestants took up definite positions." Maurois remarks, "The situation which Henry II left behind him was explosive." "Imagine a young king," wrote the Venetian ambassador, "without experience and without authority; a council rent by discord; the royal authority in the hands of a woman alternately wise, timid, and irresolute, and always a woman; the people divided into factions and the prey of insolent agitators who under pretense of religious zeal trouble the public repose, corrupt manners, disparage the law, check the administration of justice, and imperil the royal authority."

The opening, keynote chapter of J. W. Thompson's *The Wars of Religion in France, 1559-1576*, is a description of how Henry II became a one-eyed man. So we may say with fullest literal truth that the first two lines of Nostradamus' prophecy, which was first published in 1555, were most marvelously fulfilled in 1559.

The last two lines of the quatrain are as wondrous. Francis II was soon succeeded by his brother Charles IX, and he by another brother, Henry III. His concessions to the Protestants, together with his bad government and extravagance caused a reaction which brought the Duke of Guise, his party and the Holy League to the fore. The aims of the League were to maintain Catholicism, suppress Protestantism, prevent Henry of Navarre from obtaining the succession, and to restore "political rights enjoyed under Clovis." There was also a secret aim: to secure royal power for the Guise himself. The Guise highly approved.

Henry of Guise was a glamorous, popular figure: the other Henry was not. Paris was wholly devoted to the "defender of the Faith," so the King shrewdly forbade his entering the city. Yet he came. The result was that on this Day of Barricades Henry III became practically a prisoner in the Louvre. Catherine de Medici made peace between the two "They went over the past, talked of their causes for ill-will and agreed to forget them. The Duke swore fidelity and the King promised to protect the Duke." (Paul Van Dyke) Henry even offered "his old playmate of Guise" two hundred thousand scudi, but the latter would not take it till the King were better off financially.

Henry III, like a whipped cur, retired to Chartres, where he was compelled to approve all that Guise had done against him, and to grant concession after concession, including several powerful towns and making him generalissimo of the French forces. Still Guise was not satisfied. He never would be. He must be either Caesar or nothing. Henry III was the most timid of men. But now he determined to murder his rival.

From the painting by Paul Delaroche

Assassination of the Duke of Guise

"The great man of Blois will murder his friend."

The opportunity presented itself when the King convoked the Estates General at Blois. The Duke attended. The sister of de Vins, one of the leaders of the League, hearing that the Guise had dared the danger area, commented: "Since they are so near each other you will soon hear that one or the other has killed his companion." ("The Great One at Blois will kill his friend," says Nostradamus.) Historian Blair states, "He and Guise prepared for their mortal duel by receiving the Sacrament together, a custom to which the Valois were addicted when contemplating any atrocious piece of treachery." This treachery, with its feigned friendship, is dramatised magnificently in Marlowe's *Massacre at Paris*, though its author, being a Protestant,* depicts Henry III in a good light.

Enter Guise

Guise. Good morrow to your majesty.

Henry. Good morrow to my loving cousin of Guise:
How fares it this morning with your excellence?

Guise. I heard your majesty was scarcely pleas'd,
That in the court I bare so great a train.

Henry. They were to blame that said I was displeas'd;
And you, good cousin, to imagine it.
'Twere hard with me, if I should doubt my kin,
Or be suspicious of my dearest friends.
Cousin, assure you I am resolute,
Whatsoever any whisper in mine ears,
Not to suspect disloyalty in thee:
And so, sweet coz, farewell.   (*Exit with Epernoun.*)

Guise. So;
Now sues the king for favour to the Guise,
And all his minions stoop when I command:
Why, this 'tis to have an army in the field.
Now, by the holy sacrament, I swear,
As ancient Romans o'er their captive lords,
So will I triumph o'er this wanton king;
And he shall follow my proud chariot's wheels.
Now do I but begin to look about,

---

* Bacon, the concealed author of the Marlowe plays, was a Protestant. The man Marlowe was an atheist, but preferred Catholicism to Protestantism.

> And all my former time was spent in vain.
> Hold, sword,
> For in thee is the Duke of Guise's hope.

The tragedy has been many times told. Guizot relates it well:

> On the evening of Thursday, December the 22nd, the Duke of Guise, on sitting down at table, found under his napkin a note to this effect: "The King means to kill you." Guise asked for a pen, wrote at the bottom of the note, "He dare not," and threw it under the table. In spite of this warning, he persisted in going, on the next day, to the council-chamber. He crossed the king's chamber contiguous to the council-hall, courteously saluted, as he passed, Loignac and his comrades whom he found drawn up, and who, returning him a frigid obeisance, followed him as if to show him respect. On arriving at the door of the old cabinet, and just as he leaned down to raise the tapestry that covered it, Guise was struck by five poniard blows in the chest, neck, and reins: "God ha' mercy!" he cried, and, though his sword was entangled in his cloak and he was himself pinned by the arms and legs and choked by the blood that spurted from his throat, he dragged his murderers, by a supreme effort of energy, to the other end of the room, where he fell down backwards and lifeless before the bed of Henry III, who, coming to the door of his room and asking "if it was done," contemplated with mingled satisfaction and terror the inanimate body of his mighty rival, "who seemed to be merely sleeping, so little was he changed." "My God! how tall he is!" cried the King; "he looks even taller than when he was alive."

The treacherous murder shocked most of France. Whole provinces declared against Henry. The States General refused its support, so he dismissed it. The League was in arms. The Sorbonne decided that Frenchmen were released from their oath of allegiance to the King.

Up to now the civil wars had been those of "the Three Henries," but now with the Guise gone the French people had a hard choice to make of protagonists: a treacherous King who had murdered the head of the Catholic Party, or the warrior leader of the Protestant Party. Truly, as Nostradamus predicted, after the Great One of Blois murders his friend "the kingdom is put in evil and double doubt."

Note the logical relationship of the events described in this prophetic quatrain. Henry II, at a tournament, is wounded mortally in one eye and dies a few days later ("in the year" says the prophecy, most literally), this puts the court "in a very grievous trouble" (that is, the mere fact that Henry is a one-eyed king causes the trouble), Catholics and Protestants take up their positions, Henry III, son of Henry II, by his pro-Protestant policy causes the Duke of Guise to be set up by the ultra-Catholics who proves such an ambitious trouble-maker that the Great one of Blois, to make an end, "kills his friend."

Clearly, the prophet *knew* whereof he wrote.

THE MURDER AT BLOIS: PROPHECY TWO

Paris conspires to commit a great murder,
Blois will carry it into full effect:
Those of Orleans will want to set up their chief again;
Angers, Troye, Landres will do them a misdeed.

Paris conjure un grand meutre commetre,
Blois le fera sortir en plein effect:
Ceux d'Orleans voudront leur chef remettre;
Angers, Troye, Langres leur feront un meffait. (3.51)

THE MURDER PERPETRATED AT BLOIS WAS CONCEIVED IN PARIS, AS Nostradamus predicted. When Henry III learned to his dismay that Henry of Guise, with his small retinue, had reached the capital, which he had promised not to enter, the frightened monarch suggested to his mother, Catherine de Medici, that she detain the Duke as long as possible. Then he looked about for advice. "Ornano, the captain of his Corsican guards, offered to kill Guise as he entered, and a prelate, the Abbe d'Elbene, seconded the suggestion and produced Scripture to sanction it. The appropriate text occurred to him at once." (Roeder) The plan was dropped, however, as too dangerous.

After the murder of Henry of Guise at Blois Henry III despatched Balzac d'Entragues to Orleans to take over the governorship. The latter, on arrival, found himself most unwelcome, and soon was under siege in the citadel. A deputation of eight representatives of Orleans went to Blois to plead with the King, to no avail. He dismissed the deputation with, "I command you to receive and obey M. d'Entragues as your governor." After which he despatched his Swiss troops to Orleans to help the besieged Entragues.

According to *Memoirs Secret,* an anonymous pamphlet published at the time, the deputation, which stated "qu'ils auroient un autre gouverneur que monsieur d'Antragues" should have been listened to, and it was because they were not that the town so wildly welcomed the advent of their favorite, the Chevalier d'Aumales, one of the chiefs of the League. Besides, the writer argues, other cities took their example from Orleans. If the King had listened to Orleans and granted them what they wanted they would have remained obedient and so would the other towns.

Most of the cities of France rose against their King, but those that were more or less Protestant strongholds were for the harrassed monarch. Nostradamus states specifically that "Angers, Troye and Langres" will be opposed to "those of Orleans." Nostradiamian Le Pelletier, according to Ward, "says it is not very easy to distinctly prove the exact position taken up by these three towns." Apparently neither of these gentlemen, good students of the prophet though they were, knew what Nostradamus knew. According to *The Wars of Religion in France,* by J. W. Thompson, the three towns named were pro-Protestant. According to Larmor, Angers took its chateau from the Leaguers; Troyes, with Edouard Mole declared for Henry IV; and Langres let the army of the Grisons pass through. The prophecy is accurate to the letter.

THE GENTLE ASSASSIN OF THE KING-KING

The King-King not being, destroyed by the Gentle One,
The year pestilent, the seditious cloudy.
Let him hold who can, the great not joying,
And he will pass the term of the cavillers.

Le Roy-Roy n'estre, du Doux la pernicie,
L'an pestilent, les esmues nubileux.
Tien qui tiendra, les grands non letitie,
Et passera terme de cavilleux. (Presage 58)

HENRY III, WHO FOR A WHILE HAD BEEN KING OF POLAND TILL CALLED back to France on the death of his brother Charles IX, lived only seven months after he had murdered the Duke of Guise at Blois. And he was murdered because he had murdered.

Abandoned by the Catholics, Henry quickly came to terms with his brother-in-law, Henry of Navarre, and soon they were jointly besieging Paris. The Catholic League was doomed. "In desperation it betook itself to crime: preachers publicly asked if no man would avenge the murders of Blois." (Maurois) Jacques Clement, a Dominican Friar, after being assured by the theologians that a regicide could be assured of salvation when the cause was holy, managed to get to the King (August 1, 1589), handed him a letter, and while Henry was reading it, stabbed him with a poignard.

The assassin was a "Gentle One," a Friar. But "Gentle One" was also his name — Clement.

The seditious were "cloudy," confused. By all rights the Bourbon, Henry of Navarre was their legitimate King, and he had so many admirable qualities that had he not been a Protestant they would have welcomed him.

The League proclaimed one of Henry's uncles, the Cardinal de Bourbon, king; but many of the moderate Catholics went over to the Huguenot side. Henry still had a long and rough road ahead of him. "For a long time Henry had all he could do to hold his enemies in check. He had the Pope, the Emperor of Germany, the King of Spain, the Duke of Savoy, and the League, all against him. At one time he was in rags, and with hardly a horse to ride."

But "Paris is worth a mass," he is finally reported to have said, so again he turned Catholic, after which he was joyously welcomed as King by his nation. Although many of his Protestant followers were dismayed, or at least rueful, others were not. These latter were wiser. After Henry had settled down as more or less peaceful ruler of France he issued the Edict of Nantes (1598), which granted the Huguenots liberty of worship, rendered them eligible to public office, and opened the schools to their children. Thus Henry, by becoming a Catholic, was able to help the Protestants.

THE CONSPIRACY OF CINQ MARS

Old Cardinal by the young man deceived,
Will see himself disarmed out of his charge,
If, Arles, you do not reveal the duplicate;
Both Liqueduct and the Prince embalmed.

Vieux Cardinal par la jeusne deceu,
Hors de sa charge sa verra desarmé,
Arles ne monstres double soit apperceu;
Et Liqueduct et le Prince embausmé. (8.68)

CARDINAL RICHELIEU, OLD AND DYING, FOUND HIMSELF BETRAYED BY
his young protégé, twenty-year old Cinq-Mars, to the point where he
was deprived of his office and the command of the army. That perpetual
intriguer, the King's brother, Gaston d'Orleans, had won Cinq-Mars to
his will, and the latter obligingly prepared a treaty between the rebel
and the King of Spain. But their secret was betrayed; how, is not known.

States historian Patmore: "Richelieu had reached Arles when
the long-expected weapon was placed in his hands, in the shape of a
copy of the treaty concluded by the conspirators with Spain."

Liqueduct, from the Latin, means *led by water.* Nostradamus is
relevant, as usual. The dying Cardinal's memorable trip by water
is an integral part of the Cinq-Mars conspiracy story. Hilaire Belloc,
in his biography of Richelieu, writes: "In a famous picture, and in
twenty famous exercises of the pen, the tragedy has been recorded.
How the Cardinal, now far too ill to move, laboriously towed up
against the slighter summer stream of the shallow summer Rhone, having on his barge that huge purple canopy as big as a great room (where
he lay with table, chair and secretary at his side), dragged after his
craft . . . and how the two troops of cavalry followed by road
along the bank, and how, on the further shore Cinq-Mars went as a
prisoner among them."

The water-trip took Liqueduct from Tarascon to Lyons, and then
from Fontainebleau to Paris. Here Cinq-Mars was beheaded, with his
associate De Thou. The Cardinal soon followed the ungrateful delin-
quent into the next world, dying December 4, 1642. Five months later
his Prince, Louis XIII, also died. Both Cardinal and King were
embalmed.

The conspiracy of Cinq-Mars is one of the principal events of

Richelieu

"Old Cardinal by the young man deceived."

the reign of Louis XIII — or should we say, the reign of his Cardinal? Nostradamus neatly digests the story into four lines of a prophecy so precise that it cannot be misapplied to any other succession of events in history. Mention of Arles alone forbids this, particularly when conjoined with "Old Cardinal deceived by a young man, disarmed out of his charge . . . duplicate . . . Liqueduct . . . embalmed."

V

THE FRENCH REVOLUTION

"WHEN A BOUR. IS VERY BON"

When a *bour.* is very *bon*,
Bearing in himself the marks of justice,
Then bearing his name from his blood,
Through flight he will unjustly receive his punishment.

Alors qu'un bour. sera fort bon,
Portant en soy les marques de justice,
De son sang lors portant son nom,
Par fuite injuste recevra son supplice. (7.44)

W HEN a *bour.* is very *bon*" means, "When a Bourbon is very good."
Read in French the pun is obvious. It is equally obvious that it
fits no bourbon so well as France's greatest Louis.*

The great Goethe appreciated his goodness: "When a new King of
France who sought the good showed the best intentions of himself
limiting his own authority, in order to do away with numerous abuses,
achieve the finest results, and rule only for the sake of order and of
justice, the most pleasant hope spread all over the world." The English-
man, Arthur Young, traveling through France just before the Revolution, said, "The King is the honestest man in the world, with but one
wish which is to do right." May Duclaux writes that "he was well-
meaning, aimiable, full of human kindness."

---

* When Nostradamus penned this prophecy the first Bourbon kings had not
yet arrived on the throne of France.

He came to the throne at a time of enlightenment. According to the great French Historian Taine, "Never was an aristocracy so deserving of power at the moment of losing it; the privileged class, roused from their indolence, were again becoming public men, and, restored to their functions, were returning to their duties."

So the King was in a position to be able to select good men, and did so. States Guizot: "Almost the whole ministry was in the hands of reformers; a sincere desire to do good impelled the king toward those who promised him the happiness of his people."

One of the first good deeds of this *fort bon* Bourbon (achieved almost the moment he came to the throne) was to send his minister Malesherbes (an excellent man who was later guillotined with his entire family) to inspect the registers of the Bastille, which resulted in the freeing of most of its prisoners.* Then in quick succession the monarch abolished dungeons throughout the length and breadth of France, as well as the torture and the death penalty, made prison inspection mandatory five times a year, lightened penalties for all offenses, separated small offenders from criminals, introduced free circulation of grain, founded the School of Medicine in Paris, developed the ports of the realm, up-dated the Army and Navy (not for aggressive reasons but to improve the lot of the defenders of France), abolished the death penalty for deserters — not all civilized nations today have got around to this — and also the corvee (forced labor), servitude and right of *mortmaine*. He reformed the hospitals, granted full civil rights to Protestants and Jews** (1787), increased the liberty

---

* On July 14, 1789, when the yelling mob broke down the walls of the Bastille, thinking they were liberating multitudes of innocent prisoners, they found only seven inmates, namely, four forgers, two lunatics (who straightaway had to be re-incarcerated elsewhere), and a scion of the detested aristocracy, jailed by his father to cool his heels and his passions. When the mob broke in on his peace, he was just sitting down to enjoy a good dinner.

** Louis XVI has been blamed as an irresolute king, but in matters concerning the welfare of the Jews this was certainly not so. The year he ascended the throne he granted permission to Abraham Spire Levy, son of a Talmudist, to open a printery for Jewish works, particularly Talmudical. It functioned till 1794, when the Terror came. In 1776 Louis signed letters patent granting the Portuguese Jews of Bordeaux free exercise of their religion. In 1778 he suppressed anti-semitic outbreaks at Tham, Dermenach and Hagenthal in Alsace. The same year, when the orthodox Jew Cerfberr came from Strasburg to Paris to seek justice

of the press (to the point where it became license and helped bring
an end to the monarchy) and on his personal initiative renounced
his own right to impose taxes without the consent of the representatives
of the people. When in 1788, one of the worst hailstorms in history
brought about a near-famine, Louis helped alleviate it, and won
praise even from the Revolutionary journal, *Le Moniteur*: "It was
only by a sacrifice of forty millions that Louis XVI — during the

---

from an oppressive tax levied on the Jews alone, he found himself welcome at
Court, and promptly his people received the benefit of a Royal Edict against the
tax, which, in denouncing it, stated, "in assimilating the Jews to animals, this *peage
corporel* would debase humanity." The measure, however, provoked vehement
protestations on the part of the towns. Strasburg, hit in its finances, demanded
an indemnity from the King, which he granted, rather than cause trouble.
Judging that insufficient, Strasburg doubled, for the Jews, the toll for crossing
the Rhine bridge. "The King, informed, obliged the town to treat the Jews like
other passengers." Grand Rabbi Leon Berman, of Lille, whose book, *Histoire des
Juifs en France* affords the above information, in a section entitled *Bienveillance
de Louis XVI* (note the resemblance to Nostradamus' description) also relates
that in 1779, when the prosecutory tribunal of Sarraguemines attempted to expel
certain families of Frauenberg which were not on the lists of localities authorized
for the Jews, the King ordered they should stay unmolested where they were.

In 1788 Louis said one day to one of his ministers who had been selected
to carry out the recent emancipation of the Protestants, "M. de Malesherbes, you
have been made a Protestant: I am now making you a Jew." The King had just
"instituted a commission charged to study the means of ameliorating the lot of
the Jews." But, because of the outbreak of the Revolution, says Berman, "the
solution of the jewish question was retarded." Although the Republicans on
December 27, 1791 came up with a Decree of Emancipation, said emancipation
existed on paper only. The Jews had no enthusiasm for the civic oath, and no
Jews were granted positions on the Committee of General Security or the Revolutionary Tribunal. In fact, says Berman, "The Revolution bullied the believers."
In the lower Rhine the synagogues, like the churches, were transformed into
Temples of Reason. They were closed at Metz, Strasburg, Nancy, Avignon, Nimes,
Paris, Bordeaux, and St.-Esprit. At Metz the scrolls of the Law were publicly
burned. At Isle sur-Sorge the synagogue was burned down. (Quite a contrast to
the days of the Old Regime when (1780) the Princes of Bourbon and Conde
paid an honorary visit to the synagogue of Bordeaux.) The Jacobins were
strongly anti-semitic, so the usage of Hebrew was forbidden. At Saverne, three
years after the Terror, Hebrew tomb-inscriptions were defaced. The Jewish religion
was parodied and its ministers incarcerated or obliged to flee. "The true believers
could only practise their religion in secret and under the greatest precautions."
In October, 1793, Nancy forbade the Jews to engage in commerce. In 1794 the
district head of Strasburg proscribed what he called "the barbarous usages of
the Jews, and principally circumcision." Hebrew books were ordered burned,
and "First of all, the Talmud." At Bordeaux the wealth of the rich Jews was
seized. One of them (Jean de Mendes), protesting, stated he disapproved of the
Constitution for religious reasons and was promptly guillotined. Jews were guillotined in other towns, including Nimes, Lyons and Paris. Several of those executed
in the capital were considered royalists.

most distressing situation in which the finances had ever been found —
preserved France from the horrors which threatened her on all sides."
(September 16, 1789 — two months after the fall of the Bastille.) * *

Louis brought through many reforms, but not all that he wanted
to. Some were urged at too fast a pace. A chorus of protests came from
the first and second estates (nobility and clergy). Minister after
minister was dismissed. The previous king had left a mountain of
damage behind him. Had he not said cynically, "After me the de-
luge." Van Laun says, "The poor king, buffeted by so many winds,
deafened by so many shouts, dismisses Necker, as he had dismissed
Turgot." In a letter written as early as 1776 he complained to Malesherbes that he was "surrounded by men who are interested in mis-
leading my principles, and preventing the voice of public opinion
from reaching my ear." Yet he would not use force, even to establish
the good. "Despotism," he wrote again to his minister, "is good for
nothing even when employed to force the people to be happy." This
is a thought over the heads of many reformers. But Louis was also a
pacifist.

So disgusted did Louis become at having to be "a mockery king of
snow" that he even considered abdicating, and would have done so
had it been feasible. Longingly he wrote to Malesherbes: "How happy
you are. Why cannot I also quit my place?"

When the tussle arose between the first two estates and the
third over the issue of a third estate equal in size and therefore voting
power to the first two, Louis cast his vote with the minority, that is,
on the side of the people. Nostradamus was right. The Bourbon "bore
in himself the marks of justice."

He was just too in the matter of the Protestants, to whom, though
he was the devoutest of Catholics, he insisted that full civic rights should

---

* * Robert McNair Wilson, in The Mother of Napoleon, writes of Louis:
"He was a statesman much above the average in knowledge, dignity and courage . . . He was an honest and popular king who lightened the burden of the
common people, and asked sacrifices from rich land-owners . . . The pictures (of
him) presented for a century or more . . . were invented after the Revolution to
explain it." According to Saul K. Padover, the leading English-language authority
on Louis XVI, "the Revolutionary tradition libelled hs memory."

Our School history books parrot one another in telling us that Liberty,
Equality and Fraternity were won by the destruction of an absolute monarchy.
Just who brought these gifts to the French people — Marat, Danton, or Robes-
pierre?

be granted. This, and the matter of a loan, came up before the Parlement of Paris. Both matters, thought Louis, required no vote, so he ordered Parlement to register an edict only. But Parlement wanted no loan granted. Neither did it want the obnoxious measure granted of civil rights for heretics. Thus did Louis, the good Bourbon, anger and alienate Parlement and contribute to the fires of the Revolution. "Put to death on acount of his good-will," writes Nostradamus elsewhere of the good Bourbon.

When Louis heard that his brothers, who had fled to the safe far side of the Rhine were rattling their sabres loudly and urging military action against France, he wrote to rebuke them. Such a plan, he said, could be realized "only by shedding seas of blood." "You make me shudder with horror. I would rather the monarchy crumbled than that it should ever agree to such schemes." Some historians suspect the authenticity of this letter, mainly because they find it hard to conceive how a King could be willing to let his kingdom crumble in preference to going to war to defend it. But Louis' words and deeds were consistent with this document.

No better mirror of the King's mind, showing how firmly he bore within himself "the marks of justice" could be produced than the following beautiful letter written to his brother, the Count of Artois, later Louis XVIII:

September 7, 1789

My Brother,

You complain; and your letter, in which respect and fraternal affection appear to guide the pen, contains reproaches which you think well-founded. You talk of carnage, of resistance to the projects of factious men, of sovereign will . . . My brother, you are not a king! — Heaven, in placing me on the throne, gave me a feeling heart, and the sentiments of a good father. All Frenchmen are my children; and I am the common father of the great family confided to my care. Hatred and ingratitude are armed against me: but their eyes are dimmed, their judgment is bewildered; the revolutionary torrent has dizzied every brain . . . I might indeed give the signal of combat: but how horrible a combat! and how more horrible a victory! And can you believe I should have triumphed at the moment when all the orders of the state were united together, when all the people were armed against me, when all the army forgot its oaths, its honor, and its king? I might, no doubt, have given the signal of carnage; and thousands of French would have been immolated! . . . Alas! do you then appreciate as nothing the calm of a good conscience? I have done my duty, and while the assassins are the prey of remorse, I can declare loudly that I am not responsible for the blood that is shed. I have not commanded murder: I have saved the lives of Frenchmen: I have saved my family, my friends, my whole people: I have an internal conviction of having acted well, while my enemies have had recourse to crimes. Which of us is in a situation the most to be envied? Cease then, my brother, cease to accuse me: time, circumstances, and a thousand causes too long for detail, have produced the misfortunes of France. It is too cruel to reproach me with those things: this were to join with my enemies, and break my paternal heart. I have sacrificed myself, brother, for my people; and, this first duty being fulfilled be persuaded that I shall know how to sacrifice myself for you, and the Frenchmen who have followed you.

Louis bore, not only "the marks of justice" but of judgment. He was a wise man if not always a wise "ruler." When the mob first attacked the Tuileries, for instance, he put forward a suggestion which succeeded in changing the rioters into peaceful visitors. "I have had the state apartment opened," he said to them in invitation. "If the people file past on the gallery side they will enjoy seeing them." Curiosity won, and the crowd passed through the state bedroom." (Castelot)

Wisdom, judgment and goodness lived in him to the last. In his will, which he wrote on Christmas, a month before he was guillotined, he said:

I commend my children to my wife. I have never doubted her maternal tenderness for them. I charge her particularly to make of them good Christians and honest men, to make them look on the grandeurs of this world (if they should be fated to experience them) merely as dangerous and transitory advantages, and to fix their eyes on the sole reliable and lasting glory of eternity. I beg my sister to continue in her tenderness for my children and to be a mother to them if they have the misfortune to lose their own.

Among the minor indignities the good Bourbon had to suffer was that of being called by "the name of his blood," as Nostradamus prophesies. The Revolutionists would not address him as Louis XVI,

ARRESTATION DE LOUIS XVI A VARENNES (22 Juin 1791) — Violant ses serments de fidélité à la Constitution, Louis XVI s'enfuit avec la famille royale, cherchant à se réfugier à l'étranger. Reconnu par le maître de poste Drouet, il est arrêté à Varennes-en-Argonne (Meuse) et ramené à Paris.

for that would be an acknowledgement that he was King of France. To them he was Capet: which is why Nostradamus, in several of his quatrains refers to him as "the great Caped one," "esleu cap." and so on. Louis was conducted to the bar of the Convention as Louis Capet. He objected. "Capet is not my name," he said. "It is that of my ancestors."

Historian Buckley remarks: "This was not of course, and never had been, the surname of the French royal family, though its founder had been known as Hugues Capet: to call Louis XVI Capet was almost as absurd as it would be to call the present King of England Longshanks, because Edward the First was so called."

"Through flight he will unjustly receive his punishment" because of the place of *injuste* in the text-line, may be also rendered, "Through injudicious flight he will receive his punishment." Nostradamus has already described that flight, named Varennes, a journey by night by way of a forest, and even named Saulce, the oilman-grocer who detained the King and made escape impossible. And in the Gorsas-Narbon prophecy with its mention of the "red city," Nostradamus writes: "By high flight grey drape life failed."

On July 23, 1791, Louis wrote to his brother, the Count of Provence, "All thoughts of regaining the French are over . . . A few days since, I was a vain phantom of a monarch, the impotent chief of a people the tyrants of their king, and the slaves of their oppressors: I now share with them their chains. A prisoner in my palace, I am deprived even of the right of complaint . . . This flight, which was so necessary for me, which would perhaps have procured my happiness and that of my people, will furnish motives for a terrible accusation. I am menaced; the cries of hatred strike my ear. Oh! my brother! let us hope for a milder futurity: the French loved their king: what then have I done to deserve their hatred? I, who have ever borne them in my heart."

Yet Louis had words of comfort for General Bouille, who had planned and arranged the flight to Varennes and was now beating his breast in self-recriminations that all had gone awry. "Success, I know, depended on myself: but he must have an atrocious mind who could have shed the blood of his subjects, and, by making resistance, have caused a civil war in France. Those ideas rent my bosom; and all my resolution vanished. To succed I must have had the heart of Nero, and the soul of Caligula. Receive, sir, my thanks: why have I not the power to testify to you all my gratitude?"

Helen Maria Williams comments on the Varennes failure: "The greatest calamity that could have befallen the king or the country was the failure of the plan, which, had it succeeded, so far from causing a civil war, as the king seemed to fear, would have united all parties for the formation of a wiser constitution, and prevented the commission of those crimes which afterwards sullied the French revolution."

VARENNES

"VARENNES, FRANCE, 49 N. 5 E. LOUIS XVI AND HIS FAMILY CAPTURED on their flight, 1791." (Sole comment on Varennes given in Everyman's Literary and Historical Atlas of Europe. Varennes is not noted for any other event of historical importance.)

> By night he will come by the forest of Reines,*
> Married couple, devious route, Queen, the white stone,
> The monk-king in grey in Varennes.
> Elected Cap, causes tempest, fire, blood, slice.

> *De nuict viendra par le forest de Reines,*
> *Deux pars, vaultorte, Herne la pierre blanche,*
> *Le moyne noir** en gris dedans Varennes:*
> *Esleu Cap, cause tempeste, feu, sang, tranche.* (9 20)

"In the translation of this, Garencieres leaves the two words *vaultorte Herne* as in the original French, and does not attempt the translation. He also mistakes Reines for Rennes, the chief town in Little Britanny. He evidently has no conception whatever of the meaning of the quatrain. Bouys and Le Pelletier differ on minor points in rendering these words. *Forest,* Le Pelletier reads, in Latin, as *fores,* gate, that is by the Queen's gate, and he quotes Thiers to show ("Hist. Revol. Franc." 1. 309) that the Queen made sure of a secret gate out of

---

* Interpretation by Charles Ward, from "The Oracles of Nostradamus," published by Scribners.

** In the writings of Nostradamus *noir* is used as an anagram of *roi* (king) no less than 17 times.

the Tuileries, by which they escaped. But Bouys takes it for the forest of Reines, which is on the road to Varennes. *Deux pars* is husband and wife; *voltorte*, or *vaultorte*, is a crossroad, or a divergent road; it stands for the road through St. Menehould, on the way to Montmedy. This, it seems, they were forced into by posting arrangements. Prudhomme ("Revol. de Paris," No. 102, p. 542) sets the divergence down to vacillation or change of orders. If that be the correct statement, then my etymology of *face about* for *vaultorte* fits it best. *Herne* is *Reine*, by metaplasm of *h* for *i*. It was permissible in anagrammatic writing to change one letter in a word, but not more than one. The reader can refer for this to the "Dictionnaire de Trevoux," under *Anagramme*. The white stone stands for this royal or precious stone, the Queen, who was dressed in white. The King was dressed in grey. Prudhomme, in the work mentioned above (p. 554), says he wore a round hat, which hid his face, and had on an iron-grey coat *(gris de fer)* so he appeared like a Carmelite.

"De Bouille relates: The king informed me that he would leave, with his family, in a single carriage which he would have expressly for him. In the reply I made the king, I took the liberty of representing to him again that the route by Varennes offered great inconveniences, because of the relays that would be necessary . . . I then engaged His Majesty to take the route by Reims, or that of Flanders, passing by Chimay, and then traversing the Ardennes to get to Montmedy. I represented to him the inconveniences of traveling with the queen and his children, in a single carriage *faite exprès*, and which would be noticed by everybody." (Memoires, p. 217)

"The flight occured on June 20, 1791. On the following day the National Assembly suspended Louis XVI from his functions. On the 1st of September they passed another decree, that should the King surrender to the will of the people and become a Constitutional King he might do so. This he duly signed and attested on the 14th of the same month; so *Capet was elected*. The title of King of the French, instead of the King of France, had been established since October 16, 1789 ("Cyclopaedia of Universal History"), which virtually was the same thing. But yet strictly it was not until after the flight that he became *Esleu Cap*. Madame Campan, in the "Memories de Marie-Antoinette," relates that the Queen's hair had become white in a single night and she had had a lock of her white hair mounted in a ring for the Princess de Lamballe, inscribed *Blanchis par le malheur* (whitened by sorrow). She had become *la pierre plus blanche encore.* Her dress was white, and her complexion too. The *tranche* stands for the slice, or *couperet,* of the guillotine."

"PUT TO DEATH ON ACCOUNT OF HIS GOOD-WILL"

The too much good time, too much royal goodness,
Makes and unmakes, prompt, sudden, negligence,
Lightly will believe his loyal spouse false,
As for him, put to death on account of his good-will.

Le trop bon temps, trop de bonte royale,
Fais et deffais, prompt, subit, negligence,
Legier croira faux d'espouse loyalle,
Luy mis a mort par sa benevolence. (10.43)

NOSTRADAMUS, BELIEVER IN THE DIVINE RIGHT OF KINGS, YET PREDICTED that in the reign of the King "put to death on account of his good-will" there would be too much "good-time." It was so, and Pilkington in his biography of Marie Antoinette is easily able to devote an entire early chapter to "The Years of Folly."

"He makes and unmakes."* Truer of Louis XVI than of any monarch since or before the time of Nostradamus. Bouys enumerates sixty-seven ministers of Louis who took and relinquished office in eighteen years:

Amelot, Barentin, Bertrand de Molleville, Boyne, Breteuil,
Brieune, Brogli, Beaulieu, Cahier de Gerville, Calonne,
Castries, Champion de Cice, Clavieres, Chambonas, Clugny,
Dabancourt, Danton, de Grave, Delessart, de Crosne, de Joly,

---

* Marie Antoinette was also blamed. Historian Buckley says of her, "she was suspected of making and unmaking ministers."

d'Ormesson, Dabouchage, Dumourier, Duportail, Duport-
Dutertre, Duranton, Foulon, Fourguex, Fleurieres, Joly de
Flemy, Lacoste, la Galaisieres, Lailliac, la Jarre, la Luzerne,
Lamoignon, Lambert, Laporte, Latour-Dupin, Lenoir, Lian-
court, Leroux, Malesherbes, Maurepas, Miromeuil, Montmorin,
Montbarrey, Mourgues, Narbonne, Necker, Pastoret, Puysegur,
Roland, Sartines, Segur, Servan, Saint-Germain, Saint-Priest,
Sainte-Croix, Taboureau, Tarbe, Terrier-Monceil, Thevenard,
Turgot, Vergennes, Villedeuil.

Comments Charles Ward: "Several of these served twice, and
Necker was in three times; so that the number of ministries in the
time mentioned is seventy-two — a thing not to be paralleled in history
as a course of doing and undoing, of *fais and deffais*."

"He will lightly believe his loyal wife false" apparently glances
at the notorious affair of the Diamond Necklace, in which Marie Antoinette was innocently involved. For a while though, it is believed, Louis
himself lost faith in her. It is more likely, though, that the line glances
at the distrust Louis had in the queen early in his reign when he found
her too much the loyal Austrian. If she approached him when he was
reading papers of state, says Padover, he quickly covered them.

In the last line of the prophecy, *Luy*, ("As for him") is apparently
strangely and unnecessarily used. *Luy* is probably a pun on "Louis."
Regardless, the expression

put to death on account of his good-will

fits only Louis XVI among the Kings of France. His sister Elisabeth,
in almost the same words and with the identical thought, said of him,
"He will die a victim of his goodness and of his affection for his
people, for whose happiness he has never ceased to labor since his
accession to the throne." And a chapter of Maurois' *History of France*
is titled: "How, under Louis XVI, Good Will gave Birth to Weakness."

Pacifist King

After a careful study in many history books of the career of this
gentle man I have become convinced that Louis was a *pacifist King*.
This may seem a contradiction in terms. How can a king refuse to
declare war for the sake of his people and land? Perhaps he cannot
and remain a king. So let me qualify my conviction. He was a pacifist
insofar as it was humanly possible for him to be one. He would have

abdicated, had he been able to. Clery, who knew him well, said, "The brilliant prospect of power had no charms for the young Prince. He was insensible to the views of grandeur." To historian Sedillot, "By no stretch of the imagination could Louis be called a king . . . He was absolutely lost on the throne of France." The King roused wonder in Hue: "How is it that he who exerts such a command over himself should not be formed to command others?" When the evidence is accumulated, the answer is simple: he was too much a pacifist to rule.

It is true that on his ascent to the throne the young and inexperienced monarch, subject to his counsellors, had to promise aid and assistance to America, in armed rebellion against France's old foe England. Yet even this he did reluctantly, and he would not grant permission to his subjects to serve for the Colonies. Two years later he was at war with England, but only because he had drifted into it. He seemed unable to declare war. Hostilities commenced "by the natural pressure of circumstances . . . England fired the first shot on the 17th of June, 1778." Years later, as constitutional monarch under the Republican National Assembly he had to pronounce declaration of war against Austria, but he did so with a sinking heart.

On one occasion Belgium begged France for help against Austrian oppression. Louis would do nothing. Fortunately Austria soon had her hands full with Turkey and Belgium was saved. According to Van Laun, "This listlessness of France had the effect of damaging her prestige both at home and abroad. Foreigners deemed her henceforth unable of interfering in the affairs of Europe; Frenchmen were saying that their country had relapsed into the opprobious state of impotence of the Seven Years' War."

As for civil-war, "he refused to envisage it." (Joan Evans) The young Napoleon was witness to an occasion when the King refused to fire on the ringleaders of a violent mob. "A whiff of grape-shot would have taken care of everything!" was his disgusted comment. The King maintained this yielding attitude unswervingly, as a matter of pure principle. He was no vacillator or weakling, as so many historians accuse him of being. Having studied with care the history of Charles I of England, he determined to behave in every way oppositely to that unfortunate monarch. "He resisted his people: I shall not." In a letter to the Count of Artois, dated July 3, 1789, when the Capital was already in revolutionary turmoil, he rebuked his brother's belligerence: "Talk to me no more of an act of authority, of a great stroke of power: I believe it is most prudent to temporize, to yield to the storm, and expect everything from time, from ·he awakened courage of the good, and the love of Frenchmen for their king."

When Lafayette suggested to Louis that he proclaim martial law and resort to force, the King replied simply, "I do not want blood to be shed for me." And when he heard that a rabble of thousands, raging and armed with pikes, had set out on foot for Versailles, Louis wrote an extraordinary letter to the Count D'Estaing, Commander in Chief of the Versailles Militia, who had advised flight or armed resistance: "Flight would be my utter ruin. Were I to defend myself, the blood of Frenchmen would be shed. Let there be no aggression, no commotion, which can give the idea that I think of avenging or even of defending myself." (October 5, 1789) Possibly the Commander in Chief thought his King insane.

Oddly enough, his pacifism on this occasion both lost and saved lives. "The mob, which had now been joined by the National Guard of Versailles, having learned that the troops inside the palace had been forbidden to fire upon them, became more daring and began to fire on the bodyguard, wounding many and killing a few . . . Louis, meanwhile, who had heard that some of his bodyguards were being slaughtered by the mob, showed himself on a balcony and besought the people to spare them. To prove that the bodyguards would offer no armed resistance, he ordered those of them who were near him to throw their bandoleers to the people and assume the tricolor cockade; they immediately obeyed, shouting 'Long live the nation!' By this means the lives of the faithful bodyguards were saved; but the position of the royal family was as precarious as ever." (Buckley)

Two years later, when Louis with his family was captured at Varennes and brought back to Paris to his doom, the sad result was brought about by his determined pacifism. Castelot writes, "The Queen... could hear in the distance the sound of a troop of horse-men. They were the 40 hussars from Pont-de-Somme-Vesle, who had finally left their woods and swamps. With Choiseul at their head they galloped quickly down the main street, clearing the approaches to the grocery. But Louis XVI refused to order the use of force to snatch him from the hands of the municipality." Joan Evans remarks, "The king could not reconcile it with his conscience to order those loyal to him to fight a way for him over the bridge, and they could not fight without his orders." Historian Pilkington is flabbergasted at the fantastic fact: "It is almost unbelievable that Louis should have refused . . . Folly! Crass, unbelievable stupidity! Freedom was within his grasp, and

Louis let it go. All his life he had been vacillating and indecisive, and adversity had not changed him . . . Oh for a soldier, a man of action, a man who would have put aside etiquette and ceremony, a man who would have *ordered* the King into the berline there and then."

Non-resistance was deeply entrenched in his heart. After the return from Varennes, "the Queen was in despair that he made no effort to inspire or rally his followers. He refused to allow them to take possesion of the arsenal and secure the weapons stored there, for fear of provoking strife; and meanwhile the revolutionists broke into it and seized the arms." (Joan Evans) He justified his non-resistance: "It is regretted that I did not order the rebels to be attacked before they forced the arsenal . . . but what end would the attack have answered?"

Hue relates that on one occasion when Louis was threatened by an angry mob several loyal subjects desired to make a rampart around him; whereupon the King calmly ordered, "Put your swords into their scabbards. The crowd are more deceived than guilty."

When he was in the Temple prison, according to Clery, the King's valet-de-chambre, "One of the inside guards wrote on the king's door one day, and on the inside of it: 'The guillotine is permanent and awaits the tyrant Louis XVI.' The king read these words; I advanced to erase them; His Majesty objected." He was non-resistant even to offensive words scribbled on his own door. *

His old minister visited him in prison one day and informed him that an attempt would be made to rescue him on his way to the guillotine. The King would have nothing to do with such a plan. "That would compromise too many people and cause civil war in Paris; I prefer to die, and I beg you to order them from me not to make any attempt to save me. The King does not die, in France." His daughter Madame Royale later stated: "His anxiety was that he might bring the horrors of mob-violence on the head of anyone who showed himself his friend."

---

* Let none think that the King's "aversion to bloodshed" (Clery) was born of a pusillanimous nature. No braver man lived, as the historians know. He was always ready, and even desirous of meeting the mob, no matter how hostile their tempers; and yet he would not yield to their demands if he thought them unjust. He would not resist physically, but neither would he yield morally. Van Laun, in describing the attack on the Tuileries, writes: "The door was being battered by hatchets; but at the moment when the panel was about to fall, the King had it opened, and suddenly appeared before the surging mob. He simply said, 'Here I am.' His servants had to push him into the embrasure of a window, where they placed him on a chair on a table, so that he might not be trodden down by the mass . . . In justice to Louis, be it said, he did not falter for a moment, nor budge an inch face to face with this murderous crowd. He told

His anxiety was also that there might be no posthumous blood-shed through an attempt to restore his line to the throne. On the last visit he was allowed with his eight-year old boy, he said, "My son, promise me never to think of avenging my death." The Dauphin promised. Then, taking the child in his arms, he added: You have heard what I have just said but because an oath is something even more sacred than the given word, swear, lifting your hand, that you will obey your father's last wish."

Even on the scaffold, and with his last words, he prayed that his death might not result in bloodshed to his nation, his France. The Abbe Edgeworth, his confessor, relates:

> The king was obliged to lean on my arm. The difficulty with which he cilmbed made me fear for an instant that his courage was beginning to fail him; but how astonished I was when, having reached the last step, I saw him, one might say, run away from me, cross with a firm step the entire width of the scaffold, impose silence, by a single glance, to fifteen or twenty drums which were posted opposite him, and in a voice so strong that it must have been heard as far as the Pont-tour-nant, distinctly utter these ever-to-be-remembered words:

> "I die innocent of all the crimes imputed to me. I pardon the authors of my death and I pray God that the blood which you are going to spill will never fall on France . . ."

Sanson, his executioner, writing in a Paris journal, quotes this a little differently: "'I wish my blood may cement the welfare of the French.' These, citizens, are his real last words."

"Put to death on account of his good-will," wrote Nostradamus.

---

them that he would do all the Constitution permitted him to do; he put on his head a red cap tendered to him on a pike, he drank some wine from a glass offered to him by an intoxicated workman, but not for an instant did he lose his presence of mind, or the dignity the occasion required."

"UNDONE BY HIS OWN"

Death conspired will come into full effect,
Charge given and journey to death:
Elected, created, received by his own, undone.
Blood of the innocent before them in remorse.

Mort conspiree viendra en plein effect,
Charge donnee et voyage de mort:
Esleu, cree, receu par siens, deffait.
Sang d'innocent devant soy part remort. (8.87)

THE DEATH THAT BROUGHT "THE JUST ONE" TO THE GUILLOTINE WAS the fruit of hydra-headed conspiracy. The charge was imposed by the conspirators, and carried out by many who would rather the King had been banished or escaped. His people had elected him constitutional monarch, created him, and received him, and now he was undone by them. Remorse for the crime began early. "President Vergniaud, who pronounced sentence of death, passed the whole night in tears, and seemed quite in a state of despair." There was reason for remorse: the case had been prejudged. "The weakness of the prosecution's case was shown when Saint-Just was moved to exclaim that an appeal to the people would be a virtual recall of the monarchy!" (Pilkington) So there was no appeal to the people, and the journey to death in the tumbril took place. "Judicial murder had been done," writes Pilkington. "And when the noise of the cannon had died, and the beating of the drums was stilled, the people of Paris looked into their hearts and regretted this thing that had been done. In the streets and in the squares there was a kind of stupor, friends passed one another without greeting, women cried, and children ceased their noisy games. It was as if the city was in mourning."

After a painting by Raffet

Louis XVI Threatened By the Mob on Their Visit to the Tuileries

"The husband, alone, afflicted, will be mitred ... conflict will take place at the Tuileries."

Even the brutal Hebert, who in his Paris journal, *Pere Duchesne* had written so vilely of his monarch, [1] burst into sobs in the Assembly itself over his execution, and in self-defense exclaimed, "The tyrant was very fond of my dog. He often patted it. That comes to my mind now..."

However the most remarkable case of remorse expressed was that of the King's executioner. Charles-Henri Sanson was practically overwhelmed at the holy heroism of Louis on the scaffold, and to correct some false statements that had appeared in the Paris journal, *Le Thermometre du Jour,* concerning the monarch's last moments, wrote in part, in a letter published in a subsequent issue, "And, to pay regard to truth, he bore all with a coolness and firmness that astonished us all. [2] I am firmly convinced that he derived this firmness from religious principle, with which no one could seem more imbued and affected than himself."

Historian Beauchesne writes of the unhappy headsman, "He came down from the scaffold never again to ascend it. [3] The executioner was seized with remorse — a new occurrence in his fearful office, — and his remorse was so acute that it abridged his life; he died at the end of six months, directing by his will that an expiatory mass should be annually said at his expense, every 21st of January, for the repose of the soul of Louis XVI. Thus, the first attempt to expiate the murder of the 21st of January was made by the executioner.

"Does it not seem as if the will of Heaven had been that no single trait of resemblance should be wanting between the royal martyrdom and that of our blessed Lord? The King's clothes were divided after his death like the garments of Christ; and Sanson, performing, after his manner, the part of the centurion, withdrew, after the execution, beating his breast, and repeating, 'Vere hic homo erat justus.' "

---

[1] He said, "I took delight in examining the wild beasts . . . Picture to yourself the Rhinoceros, foaming with rage at finding himself enchained, and panting with the thirst for blood with which he is devoured. There you have, feature for feature, the resemblance to Louis the Traitor, snoring at night like a swine on its dung-heap."

[2] Garat, Minister of Justice, who informed Louis XVI of the sentence of death, said his fortitude had something in it supernatural.

[3] His son Henri, who took over his office, after his father's death, saw to it the services were continued, which they were till his own death in 1840. Thus long their remorse lasted.

"IN THE SOIL THE FACE ANOINTED WITH MILK AND HONEY"

By great discord the whirlwind will tremble,
Broken accord, raising the head to heaven,
Bloody mouth will swim in its own blood,
In the soil the face anointed with milk and honey.

Par grand discord la trombe tremblera,
Accord rompu, dressant la teste au ciel,
Bouche sanglante dans le sang nagera,
Au sol la face oingte de laict et miel. (1.57)

WHEN THE GOOD BOURBON WAS GUILLOTINED THE WHIRLWIND OF THE
Revolution itself trembled, then and much more thereafter. Though the
sansculotte (breechless) rabble ridiculously called Louis tyrant, they
themselves were the tyrants with the opportunist thugs they let lead
them. Fear was supreme lord, which reached its peak in the days of the
Terror and its pilot, the all-suspicious Robespierre. When heads were
finally falling at the rate of two hundred a week the trembling of the
whirlwind informed every atom. But the disease forced its cure, the
monsters too were made to attend Madame Guillotine's "red mass," and
when the head of *Renard* bit the dust the Terror came to a sudden
and almost universally desired end. Such were a few of the fruits of
the broken accord, — broken not by Louis, but by the Republicans,
who were not loyal to the Constitution.

"The face anointed with milk and honey" (from the sacred
ampulla) was that of the Lord's anointed, Nostradamus' King to be.
But now it is in the soil, with bloody mouth and swimming in blood.
Broken accord raised not only its own head to heaven but that of the
King. Moments after the guillotining executioner Sanson picked up
Louis' bloody head by the hair and held it in the air for all to see,
a sweet sight for all foes of decency.

That excellent Nostradamian James Laver points out a curious
historical fact: "During his last moments Louis was actually reciting
the fourth verse of the Third Psalm: *Domine gloria mea et exaltans
caput meum* (Thou, O Lord, art my glory, and the lifter up of mine
head.)" What is even more remarkable: "The face anointed with
milk and honey (i.e. at the Coronation) lies on the ground. The Office

of St. Agnes, contains the words: *Mel* (honey) *et lac* (milk) *ex ore ejus* (mouth) *suscepi, et sanguis* (blood) *ejus ornavit oras* (face) *meas . . ."*

Louis XVI was guillotined January 21.

The Feast of St. Agnes is January 21.

"THE CITY OF THE BLADE BURNS THE FACE WITH POWDER"

Prince of very comely beauty,
Led to the head, made second, betrayed.
The city of the blade burns the face with powder,
Because of too great a murder the head of the King hated.

Prince de beaute tant venuste,
Au chef menee, le second faict, trahy.
La cite au glaive de poudre face aduste,
Par trop grand meurtre la chef du Roi hay. (6.92)

TO NOSTRADAMUS AND TO SOME HISTORIANS LOUIS XVI WAS "OF VERY comely beauty." To others he was not. His valet-de-chambre, Clery, wrote of him:

The unfortunate Monarch was endowed with a good constitution, and with an extraordinary share of bodily strength. His height was five feet ten inches. He carried his head with dignity. His forehead was large, and his features strongly marked; he had rather a downcast, though a steady look. His eyes were blue and large, he had full cheeks, a well proportioned mouth and regular teeth; his lips were somewhat thick, like those of most of the Bourbons, and his skin remarkably white. In the latter years of his life he grew rather corpulent, but this *embonpoint* became him, and gave to his gait a degree of firmness equally remote from awkwardness and negligence.

Louis XVI was "led to the head" in 1774, year of his accession, but "made second" when, on the 14th of July, 1790, the first anniversary of the taking of the Bastille, he did an unprecedented thing for a French monarch by ratifying the recently drawn up Constitution, and then, in the presence of an immense multitude taking an oath to maintain the liberties of the people under the Constitution.

His betrayal by "The City of the Blade" soon followed. *Glaive* is, specifically, a one-edged blade, such as was used for the guillotine. After the crime of killing the King — "too great a murder" — the City of the Blade, to obliterate the hated remains threw them in a grave lined with quicklime, then sprinkled them with more of the powder till they were covered. "When the grave was reopened some twenty-four years after, to bestow a more decent burial on the relics, nothing remained but a few fragments of calcined bone."

The two "King's head" quatrains may be read together as one prophecy. Which done we find Nostradamus telling us of something that was unthinkable in his time: A King beheaded, and his head burned with powder. And in the same quatrain words are quoted that are found in a religious service performed on January 21, the day France's greatest Louis was guillotined.

"THE QUEEN SENT TO DEATH BY JURORS CHOSEN BY LOT"

The government taken over will convict the King,
The queen sent to death by jurors chosen by lot,
They will deny life to the Queen's son,
And the prostitute shares the fate of the consort.

Le regne prins le Roy convicra,
La dame prinse a mort jures a sort,
La vie a Royne fils on desniera,
Et la pellix au sort de la consort. (9.77)

HERE IS A THUMB-NAIL PROPHECY OF THE FATE OF FRANCE'S ROYAL family. The quatrain cannot properly be applied to any other set of historical facts than those it so obviously portrays. The government was taken over by the reds of the Revolution, the King was guillotined, the queen was sent to death by jurors chosen by lot — the only queen

in history to whom this happened* — and her son the Dauphin was
badly treated and neglected, till he died of sickness and malnutrition.
Madame du Barry, mistress of the preceding king, and Marie Antoinette's old enemy**, shared the fate of the Queen. She was guillotined
for helping emigres get out of the country.

"THE PUBLIC SAINT"

Renard will be elected, not sounding a word,
Playing the public saint, living on barley bread,
After a while to tyrannize,
Setting his foot on the throat of the greatest.

Esleu sera Renard, ne sonant mot,
Faisant le saint public, vivant pain d'orge,
Tyranizer apres tant a un cop,
Mettant a pied des plus grands sur la gorge. (8.41)

"FROM A HUMBLE MEMBER OF THE STATES-GENERAL OF 1789," SAYS
David Montgomery of Maximilien Robespierre, "he had risen in a little
more than five years to be an absolute ruler, more despotic than any
of the Bourbon kings had dared to be." So he tyrannized "after a while,"
as Nostradamus writes. Was he also a fox, as the quatrain indicates?
Indeed he was. He wanted to get rid both of his old companion Danton
and the atheist-hypocrite Hebert. So he chose Hebert as first victim
"because Danton, the stronger of the two, could help.him to destroy
Hebert."

Did he "play the public saint"? According to Thibaudeau, "There
dwelt within him something of Mahomet and of Cromwell." "And this

* According to Ward and Le Pelletier, "The judgment upon Marie Antoinette was passed by the *Tribunal revolutionnaire*, newly set up, which pro-
ceeded by jurors chosen by lot, *jures a sort.*"
** A whole chapter of Pilkington's Queen of Trianon is devoted to their
enmity.

Mahomet was ambitious to be Allah. Saint-Just, who idolized him, wrote to him: 'You whom I know, like God, through prodigies alone . . ."' (Maurois) He ordered a Feast of the Supreme Being at which an Opera choral group sang "Father of the Universe, Supreme Intelligence . . ." and he read a sermon. "During this weird ceremony you might briefly have wondered whether he were the priest or the idol." (Maurois) "Atheism is aristocratic," said the dictator. "The idea of a Great Being who watches over innocence and punishes triumphant crime, is entirely popular." He made such a thundering denunciation of the ridiculous and vile anti-Christian campaign that Hebert squirmed and in the next issue of his atheist journal paid homage to Christianity. But it was too late!

Nostradamus characterizes the regicide as "not sounding a word." Robespierre was feared for his ominous silences. No one knew where he was going to strike next. Carlyle was impressed by his moody taciturnity: "The Incorruptible himself sits apart; or is seen stalking in solitary places in the fields, with an intensely meditative air; some say, 'with eyes red-spotted,' fruit of extreme bile: the lamentablest seagreen Chimera that walks the Earth that July! . . . What his thoughts might be? His plans for finishing the Terror? One knows not . . . So stalks he, this poor Robespierre, like a seagreen ghost, through the blooming July. Vestiges of schemes flit dim. But *what* his schemes or his thoughts were will never be known to man."

"Living on barley bread" says Nostradamus, indicating that the tyrant is an ascetic and Puritan. "A strict code of morality was generally added, especially by the group represented by Robespierre. Under the Robespierrist Commune prostitution was suppressed, salacious pictures were banned, and soldiers were forbidden to bathe in the Seine where they might be seen. The Robespierrists set a high value on frugality . . . The virtues of democracy in those days were austere." (R. R. Palmer) Carlyle writes his epitaph with a whit of admiration: "Stricter man, according to his Formula, to his Credo and his Cant, of probities, benevolences, pleasures-of-virtue, and such like, lived not in that age. A man fitted, in some luckier settled age, to have become one of those incorruptible barren Pattern- Figures, and have had marble-tablets and funeral-sermons. His poor landlord, the cabinet-maker in the Rue Saint-Honore, loved him; his Brother died for him. May God be merciful to him, and to us!"

It is a curious fact that after he had shot off his cheek to forestall the guillotine by suicide, "he was laid on a table, his head resting on a box of samples of army bread." (Palmer)

THE REDS OF THE FRENCH REVOLUTION

IT IS NOT HARD TO INTERPRET THE QUATRAINS OF NOSTRADAMUS REFER-ing to the man "covered with the great cape." Any French historian can know who is meant. According to the Larousse Dictionary:

> *Capet* signifies *covered with a cape* (Vetu d'une *cape* ou *chappe*). This is the name under which Louis 16 was officially designated, after the revolution of August 10, 1792, by appli-cation of the decrees which obliged the nobles to give up their feudal name to retake their primitive family name.

When Austria invaded France, King Louis' doom was sealed. "The fatherland is in danger!" was the cry. The Revolutionists feared that royalty might aid the invader and thus mar or end the success of the Revolution. Hence a "Committee of Twelve" was organized with legis-lative powers, and constituted itself a Committee of Public Safety. A Manifesto was addressed to the King, which stated:

> "The Nation will no doubt be able to defend and preserve its liberties alone, but it calls on you, Sire, *for the last time*, to join in the defence of the Constitution and the throne!"

Thus was "the Cape" soiled, and later it was stained with the blood of its royal owner. Nostradamus foresaw this in the 16th century:

> He who will have been covered with the great cape
> Will be induced in some measure to prepare:
> The Twelve Reds will come to soil the cloth,
> Under murder, more murder will be perpetrated.

> *Celuy qu'aura couvert de la grand cappe,*
> *Sera induit a quelque cas patrer;*
> *Les douze rouges viendront souiller la nappe,*
> *Subs meurtre, meurtre se viendra perpetrer.* (4.11)

Historian Madelin states that the Girondins (moderate reds) "really desired to save the King. But to this battle they marched without discipline." They failed tragically. Three out of four of the royal family were put to death: King Louis, Queen Marie Antoinette, and the Dauphin. Madame Royal, the king's daughter, lived to tell the terrible tale. The Jacobins (extreme reds) pursued the moderate reds to the death, guillotining most of their leaders, hunting others down like dogs, with the vengeful cry, "The traitors wished to save the King!" Nostradamus summarizes:

> To sustain the great troubled Cape,
> To clear him the reds will march:
> The family will be almost overwhelmed by death,
> The red reds will overwhelm the red.

> *A soustenir la grand cappe troublee,*
> *Pour l'esclaircir les rouges marcheront,*
> *De mort famille sera presque accablee,*
> *Les rouges rouges le rouge assommeront.* (8.19)

Another prophetic quatrain involving the reds of the Revolution is so clear as to hardly require interpretation. In it *the whirlwind* is the all-uprooting terror that came when the new men seized power, and *the litter* is the vehicle used to carry the nobility.

When the litter is overturned by the whirlwind,
And men's faces are covered with their cloaks,
The republic will be vexed by new men,*
Then whites and reds will judge from opposing standpoints.

Quand la lictiere tourbillon versee,
Et seront faces de leurs manteux couvers,
La republique par gens nouveaux vexee,
Lors blancs et rouges jugeront a l'envers. (1.3)

To such an extent did the "red reds overwhelm the red" that in the end no one was left but the extremest red of all, the bloody Robespierre, in his early days a foe of capital punishment but in power a tyrant clamoring for more and more blood and not nearly satisfied

---

* Louis, in 1792, wrote, "I have purchased dearly enough, sir, the right of mistrusting those new men, eager for power, and impatient to act a brilliant part."

by even two hundred guillotined heads a week. Everyone shuddered. No one knew when his turn might come. Finally reds and red-reds, and he too was forced to step to the guillotine.

But what irony! Though with Robespierre's fall peace came, a new type of tyranny was soon to arise, one more glamorous, but none the less bloody. Napoleon, "the child of the Revolution," bathed the nations in blood.

> Against the reds sections will band,
> Fire, water, iron, cord will be undermined by peace,
> Brought to death those who machinated,
> Except one who will bring ruin on all the world.
>
> *Contre les rouges sectes se banderont,*
> *Feu, eau, fer, corde, par paix se minera,*
> *Au point mourir ceux qui machineront,*
> *Fors un que monde sur tout ruynera.* (9.51)

Note how Nostradamus uses the term *reds,* — as we do today. He opposes reds to red reds, he opposes reds and whites, he associates reds with undercover activity, with "the republic," with an uprooting whirlwind, with ever more and more perpetration of murder, with an attack on "the caped one" (identified by Larousse with Louis XVI), with the murder of most of his family, with an autocracy of "twelve reds," with a reaction against the reds, and a peace followed by the appearance of one who ruins the world.

TERROR AT NANTES

AMONG THE PREDICTIONS OF THE 16TH CENTURY FRENCH SEER ARE MANY on the fate of his beloved France during the Revolution. Here is one:

> The principal citizens of the city in revolt,
> Who will make a strong stand to recover their liberty;
> Males beheaded, an unhappy melee,
> Cries, howlings at Nantes, piteous to see.

> *Des principauz de cite rebellee,*
> *Quite tiendront fort pour liberte r'avoir,*
> *Detranches masles, infelice meslee,*
> *Cris, hurlements, a Nantes piteux voir!* (5.33)

Nantes is celebrated in history for the infamous *Noyades (drownings)* and other atrocities committed therein by Revolutionist Carrier, *"not to be forgotten for centuries,"* as Carlyle says.

Nostradamus, in the prophecy above, is precise as usual. First he describes Nantes as "the city in revolt." So it was. In 1793 it became the focus of the Vendean reaction against the Republic. Such "a strong stand to recover liberty" was made by these ignorant peasants that in the next century Honore de Balzac felt inspired to write a novel about it — his celebrated *Les Chouans*. With magnificent resistance the plucky Vendeans defeated Westermann, the new generals of the Republic, and even the regular French troops under Kleber. They neither gave nor asked quarter — and they received none. But after much bloodshed the revolt was quelled and Nantes invested by the Terror. The cruel Carrier was sent to the unhappy city to punish the rebels, and what he did there was enough to rejoice the heart of a Heydrich. According to Mignet, "He had only awaited the opportunity to execute enormities that the imagination even of Marat would not have dared to conceive. Sent to the borders of an insurgent country, he condemned to death the whole hostile population — priests, women, children, old men, and girls."

Nostradamus singles out for special mention, "The principal citizens." So does historian Matthews: "Then Carrier attacked the bourgeoisie, and 325 persons, including most of the old officers of the region and 132 prominent and wealthy citizens, were sent to the Revolutionary Tribunal at Paris."

"The males beheaded," headlines the French prophet. How precise! Not merely the men were so treated. Carlyle writes, "Little children are guillotined, and aged men. Swift as the machine is, it will not serve; the headsman and all his valets sink worn down with work; declare that the human muscles can do no more."

Fusillading followed. "Prisoners who had actually borne arms against the Republic, to the number of at least 1,800, were shot in batches, utterly without trial." But this was too slow, hence the infamous *Noyades,* or "drownings," a black brain-child of Carrier. Twenty-five there were. Carlyle paints the first of them:

"Why unmoors that flatbottomed craft, that *gabarre;* about eleven at night; with ninety priests under hatches? They are going to Belle Isle? In the middle of the Loire stream, on signal given, the gabarre is scuttled; she sinks with all her cargo. 'Sentence of deportation,' writes Carrier, 'was executed vertically.' The ninety priests, with their gabarre coffin lie deep!"

But even this was too slow. Consequently, many men and women were stripped naked, tied together in pairs (humorously styled "Republican Marriages") and hurled into the River Loire, with the jeers and roars of laughter of the Reds ringing in their ears. Remember, was not the entire population to be systematically wiped out? Writes Carlyle bitterly:

"Why waste a gabarre, sinking it with them? Fling them out; fling them out, with their hands tied; pour a continual hail of lead over all the space, till the last struggler of them be sunk! Unsound sleepers of Nantes, and the sea-villages thereabouts, hear the musketry amid the night winds; wonder what the meaning of it is. And women were in the gabarre; whom the Red Nightcaps were stripping naked; who begged in their agony, that their smocks might not be stripped from them. And young children were thrown in, their mothers vainly pleading: 'Wolfings,' answered the Company of Marat, 'who would grow to be wolves.' "

In a little over a month "the mouth of the river was stopped with corpses," and thousands of the inhabitants of Nantes perished in pestilence arising from the stench of the putrefying bodies.

Cries Carlyle: "Hearest thou not, O reader (for the sound reaches through centuries), in the dead December and January nights, over

Nantes town — confused noises, as of musketry and tumult, as of rage and lamentation; mingling with the everlasting moan of the Loire water there? . . . not to be forgotten for centuries."

And Nostradamus too heard the "unhappy melee" (for the sound reaches through centuries, in both directions), so he penned in sorrow:

"Cries and howlings at Nantes — piteous to see!"

TWO QUATRAINS ON LOUIS XVIII

1. Learned and Debonnaire

The inhuman tyrant will die a hundred times;
Put in his place learned and debonnaire:
All the senate will be under his hand,
He will be grieved by a bold criminal.

Cent fois mourra le tyran inhumain;
Mis a son lieu scavant et debonnaire:
Tout le senat sera dessous sa main,
Fasche sera par malin temeraire. (10.90)

NAPOLEON, THE INHUMAN TYRANT, DIED A HUNDRED DEATHS: AT ELBA;
then, after his brief glory of a hundred days, at Waterloo; then again
at St. Helena, where he regretted the past while dying slowly of cancer
of the stomach.

The debonnaire Louis XVIII followed him. The learning of this
cheerful brother of the unfortunate Louis XVI was a byword. "He was
regarded as the clever one of the family. At fifteen he knew Latin and
had a smattering of several other languages; his tutors observed that
he was particularly fond of the moral side of history." (Lucas-Dubreton) He liked to surround himself with men of letters. Even his valet
Arnauld was a gifted poet "and future member of the French Academy,
while his *intendant* Morel was a writer of opera librettos."

Both houses of parliament ("all the senate") were under his hand. His latter life was happy but he was grieved by the bold criminal Louvel (See page 60).

2. Too Much Faith in Kitchen

Happy in the reign of France, happy in life,
Ignorant of blood, death, fury and rapine,
By flattering name will be held in longing:
King withdrawn, too much faith in kitchen.

Heureux au regne de France, heureux de vie,
Ignorant sang, mort, furer & rapine,
Par nom flatteur sera mis en envie:
Roy desrobe, trop de foye en cuisine. (10.16)

LOUIS XVIII HAD ESCAPED THE VIOLENCE OF THE REVOLUTION WHICH guillotined his sister and brother, and unlike his immediate predecessor on the throne, he was "ignorant of blood, death, fury and rapine." His biographer, Lucas-Dubreton, states, "He averted the calamity which threatened the country and left France rich, orderly and at peace with Europe." Thiers called him "the best of our constitutional kings." Maurois says, "Louis XVIII, son of France, believed in his rights, but he wanted a quiet reign, loved peace, classical tags, and risque stories, and understood that he could retain his throne only by accepting the ideas of his subjects. Absolute monarchy seemed to him desirable, but out of the question; from this arose his firm intention of abiding by the Charter."

He was known to people as *"Le Desire,"* so by "flattering name" was "held in longing." He was a king "withdrawn." "He seldom went out hunting in the neighborhood of Versailles; he preferred to sit in his library talking quietly, discussing with subtlety one of Horace's odes or one of Quinault's tragedies." (Lucas-Dubreton)

He had much "too much faith in kitchen." "His appetite and his thirst were enormous, worthy of Louis XIV in his prime: he consumed $7\frac{1}{2}$ litres of wine daily, and his bakery, cellar, kitchen and utensils cost an average of 1382 livres a day. His bill of fare was stupendous, though the items of which it consisted would make a gourmet's mouth water. It is not surprising that from his youth up he was stout, more or less gouty, and notoriously plethoric." (Lucas-Dubreton)

The two thoughts that Nostradamus juxtaposes about him in the last line of the quatrain, "King withdrawn, too much faith in kitchen," are brought together in the same way by his biographer Lucas-Dubreton: "He lived the life of an epicure, chiefly interested in food and books; he was said to be dividing his time between sumptuous repasts and a great work on natural philosophy."

THE EMPRESS EUGENIE

Of weak land and poor parentage,
By aim and peace will attain to the Empire,
Young female, reigning long time,
So that one so bad never arrived to the kingdom.

De terre foible et pauvre parentelle,
Par bout et paix parviendra dans l'empire,
Long temps regner une jeune femelle,
Qu'oncques en regne n'en survint un si pire. (3.28)

IN 1853 THE EMPEROR, NAPOLEON III MARRIED THE YOUNG AND BEAUTIFUL Spanish girl, Eugenie de Montijo, of slight estate and poor but noble parentage. "It was said of her that she began by being the futile woman and ended by being the fatal woman — a harsh witticism, but by and large a true one." (Maurois)

Eugenie had elected Marie Antoinette as her heroine and pattern . . . She had spirit, like a thoroughbred; but spirit is not a substitute for mind. In public affairs, she believed in a haughty, truculent attitude, which she mistook for firmness and energy; and she used the same forcible methods in private life. The Tuileries resounded at times with her angry voice — a courtier or a flunky behind every door. She threatened, and caused, scandal: she rushed away in a rage, once as far as Scotland in the wrong season, once to Schwalbach near Wiesbaden. Napoleon could face physical danger, without bravado but with stolid courage; he found it harder to face conjugal scenes . . .

Her official status justified her in bursting in upon cabinet meetings. But apart from these spasmodic activities, she exerted an insidious, incessant pressure upon the Emperor. There is no definite act, not even the declaration of war in 1870, for which she can be made solely responsible . . . She placed the prestige of the dynasty above the interests of the nation. (Albert Guerard)

VI

PROPHECIES ON THE 20th CENTURY

THE RUSSIAN REVOLUTION

Songs, chants and slogans of the Slavic people
While princes and Lord are captive in the prisons,
In the future, by idiots without heads
Will be received as divine oracles.

De gent esclave chansons, chants et requestes
Captifs par Princes et Seigneur aux prisons,
A l'advenir par idiots sans testes
Seront receus par divines oraisons. (1.14)

THIS prophecy is so clear as to need no interpretation. What is worthy of note, however, is that Nostradamus, who devotes so many quatrains to the French Revolution, considers the Russian Revolution of much less importance. Very few of his quatrains concern the Soviet New Order. Also, his attitudes towards the two revolutions are contrasting. In describing the French Revolution his feelings, where expressed, evince unmitigated horror, but towards the Russian Revolution and its fruits his feelings are only of scorn.

The paucity of prophecies on Communism would indicate that Soviet Russia is not long to be a "troubler of the poor world's peace."

FIVE QUATRAINS ON WORLD WAR TWO

1. The Blockade of Britain

Those in the Isles a long time besieged
Will take vigor and strength against their enemies:
Those outside, dead with hunger, overthrown,
They will never be placed in a hunger to compare with it.

Ceux dans les isles de long temps assiegez
Prendront vigueur force contre ennemis
Ceux par dehors mort de faim profligez,
En plus grand faim que jamais seront mis. (3.71)

UNLESS OTHERWISE INDICATED, REFERENCES TO "THE ISLES," IN NOSTRA-
damus, are always to the British Isles.

When France fell in June, 1940, many believed that those in the
Isles were doomed. But they were not. Slowly and painfully, England
won strength. Every day and in every way the R.A.F. grew stronger
and stronger and its bombing raids longer and longer. But those
outside the British Isles, on the continent of Europe, were still overthrown, and their hunger increased daily.

As long as those poor unfortunates continued to feel the vile yoke
of the Nazis their hunger continued to increase. Relief from hunger
came only with relief from Hitler.

2. Castulon Is Curbed

The Italian land will tremble near the mountains,
England and France will not be too well confederated,
They will help each other because of fear,
Only Castulon and the French will be curbed.

Terre Italique pres monts tremblera,
Lyon et Coq non trop confederez,
En lieu de peur l'un l'autre s'aidera,
Seul Castulon et Celtes moderez. (1.93)

Very violently did the Italian land tremble near the mountains
when on March 12, 1938, the heavy-heeled goose-steppers of Der

Fuehrer tramped into Austria. Four months later the King of England significantly paid a good-will visit to France. Less than a year later the Cock and the Lion (and the Bear!) signed a non-aggression pact. On September 3, 1939, Britain and France declared war on Germany, but by June of the following year the alliance was at an end, with France curbed by the Nazi victors. Even the stirring Revolutionary slogan of "Liberty, Equality, Fraternity," was lost to the French. It is *this* Liberty that Nostradamus seems to have in mind, for in the original text the word is "Castulon,"* *i.e.,* "castula," the Roman tunic worn by the Republican goddess of Liberty.

3. France Conquered From Within and Without

The machines of flying fire
Will come to worry the great commander of the besieged:
Inside there will be such sedition,
That the overthrown will be in despair.

De feu volant la machination
Viendra troubler au grand chef assiegez:
Dedans sera telle sedition,
Qu'en desespoir seront les profligez. (6.34)

"Inside," means "inside the city," and the city is always Paris unless the quatrain signifies otherwise, which it does not.

Some have interpreted "the machines of flying fire" as aeroplanes, but Nostradamus does not say so, and unless he does say so there is no reason for assuming such a far-fetched meaning. The prophet is quite capable of describing air-war. Elsewhere he writes:

Because of the Germans, they and their neighbors around them
Will be in wars for control of the clouds. (5.85)

and

The armies will fight in the sky for a long time. (3.11)

Here he simply mentions "machines of flying fire," describing the fire as flying, not the machines.

Such machines were employed by the Germans to break Belgian

---

* Elsewhere Nostradamus writes: "Outre la course du Castulon monarque" (1.31).

and French resistance. *The N. Y. Times* for May 14, 1940, gives this front-page item:

> Germany's newest implement of war, as terrifying as the Stuka dive bombers, appeared on the Western Front today, when flame-throwing tanks operated by men swathed in asbestos were said to have swept through Flanders villages toward the English Channel.
>
> The tank rolls up to a building and sets it afire by squirting flaming gasoline inside.

Nostradamus and *Time Magazine* make almost identical comments:

Nostradamus

The machines of flying fire
Will come to worry the great commander of the besieged.

Time Magazine, June 3, 1940

> Last week's situation was fraught with distractions to worry a commander on an unparalleled scale . . . German motorcycle troops with armored breastplates and flame-throwing tanks with crews in suits of asbestos made incursions behind the French lines.

According to a United Press report 2250 tanks were used against France. Many of these were of the flame-throwing variety.

Thus did Paris fall, flame-throwing tanks without, and sedition within, leaving the overthrown in despair.

4. "A Doddering Old Man Will Arise"

An old man with the title of chief will arise, of doddering sense,
Degenerating in knowledge and arms:
Head of France (feared by his sister),
The country divided, conceded to gendarmes.

D'un chef vieillard naistra sens hebete,
Degenerant par scavoir et par armes:
Le chef de France par sa soeur redoute,
Champs divisez, concedez aux gens d'armes. (1.78)

Nostradamus does not call this old man "king" of France, but "head" (*chief*).

"Feared" is the most obvious translation of "redoute," though the word may mean simply, *held in awe,** dislike, or distaste.*

The doddering old man, with the title of chief (Marshal), *had* a sister-in-law. French-born Marie Terese Petain was married to a Texas physician and was living in this country. *Time Magazine* (July 1, 1940) reported her as saying that the Marshal should not be head of France, as he is much too old (84). Apparently then she feared him as head of France and feared for France as well. Her comment is identical in substance with that of Nostradamus as expressed in the first two lines of this prophecy.

"Degenerating in knowledge in arms" indicates that the doddering old man was once "valiant in arms." Certainty he was made puppet head of France not only because of his pro-fascist leanings, but because the Germans considered it good policy to place a man in power who had been one of France's greatest heroes in the first World War.

The country was divided up into occupied and unoccupied France and was in the hands of "gendarmes" or military police.

Since this prophecy was written it is referable to no head of France but Petain.

5. Failure Of The Maginot Line

Near the great river great retrenchment, earth withdrawn,
It will be divided by the water into fifteen sections:
The city will be taken, fire, blood, cries, all turmoil,
And the greater part of the people confused by the shock.

Pres du grand fleuve grand fosse, terre egeste,
*En quinze parts l'eau sera divisee:**
La cite prinse, feu, sang, cris, conflit meste,
Et la plus part concerne au collisee. (4.80)

Two years before the second World War there appeared a text

---

* Froissart writes, "Noz redoubtees demoiselles"

* Literally, "The water will be divided into fifteen sections," but the sentence order in the French is inverted and the "de" (by) elided. Obviously it is the trench (*near* the river) which is divided, as one would not divide the river into fifteen sections by a trench, but vice versa.

on the prophecies of Nostradamus, written by the French scholar Fontbrune. His comment on the present prophecy is interesting: he knew that the first half of the quatrain was an accurate description of the Maginot Line, and that the last half predicted the retrenchment would fail to keep the enemy from the gates of Paris.

Map of the Maginot Line showing its hydrographic division into fifteen sections. The "great river" is the Rhine.

When Fontbrune wrote his book it was not generally believed by military authorities that the great Line would fail in the hour of need. On the contrary, they and the democratic press were constantly dinning it into our minds that it was a superlative triumph of engineering skill and therefore impregnable. Gradually the famous Maginot Line mentality was built and a false security created among the French. In June, 1940, the great trial came, the military experts were proved wrong, and Nostradamus and Monsieur Fontbrune right.

Perhaps the Maginot Line, considered on its own merits, *was* impregnable. But the military experts left out of their calculations the human element: if the great barrier was impregnable the people were not. Their minds were filled with confusion and defeatism, not fortified against the evil to come; there was treachery aplenty, as the French themselves have been the first to admit; they were morally unprepared.

It should have been obvious that even a dozen Maginot Lines are of no avail if there is confusion, defeatism and treachery *behind* the lines.

PROPHECIES OF INVENTIONS

THE PERISCOPE

FOUR TIMES THE SIXTEENTH CENTURY FRENCH SEER PROPHESIES THE submarine. Three of the prophecies remain unfulfilled, but the other apparently forecast Hitler's failure to prevent American lend-lease supplies from reaching the British. In the following quatrain, the "eye of the sea" is the periscope:

> From where he thought to cause famine to come,
> From there will come abundance of supplies.
> The eye of the sea watches like a greedy dog,
> While one gives the other oil, wheat.

> *D'ou pensera faire venir famine,*
> *De la viendra le rassassiement.*
> *L'oeil de la mer par avare canine,*
> *Pour de l'un l'autre donra huille froment.* (4.15)

The following quatrain describes a submarine not yet invented, an amphibian, which serves as a tank on the land. Its appearance is "strange," which it would be to one living in the 16th century and will be to us; it is "pleasing," because a machine able to speed through sea and land would be streamlined; it is "terrible" because it can approach under water and appear unexpectedly for a blitzkrieg.

When the terrestrial and aquatic fish
Is set on the shore by the strong wave,
Its form strange, pleasing, and yet terrible,
Then the enemy will come from the sea and soon reach the walls.

Quand le poisson terrestre & aquatique
Par forte vague au gravier sera mis,
Sa forme estrange suave & horrifique,
Par mers aux murs bien tost les ennemis. (1.29)

In one quatrain Nostradamus envisions a whole fleet of submarines:

By lightning on the arch, gold and silver melted,
Of the two captives the one will eat the other
Of the most widely extended city,
When the fleet can swim under water.

Par foudre en l'arche or & argent fondu,
De deux captifs l'un l'autre mangera
De la cite le plus grand estendu,
Quand submerge la class nagera. (3.13)

Except for the remarkable last line, no part of the prophecy is clear, unless "the most widely extended city" refers to London. The events have not yet begun to come to pass.

THE SUBMARINE

In the next prophecy quoted, the fish described is obviously a submarine, since it is used for making war, and a fleet commander comes out of it:

When there is iron and a letter enclosed in a fish,
He who will then make war will go out from it,

He will have his fleet well rowed through the sea,
Appearing near the Latin land.

Qu'en dans poisson, fer & lettre enfermee,
Hors sortira, qui puis fera la guerre,
Aura par mer sa classe bien ramee,
Apparoissant pres de Latine terre. (2.5)

THE AIRPLANE

In another quatrain the far-sighted Frenchman sees both sub-marines and airplanes:

The scourges past, the world diminished,
For a long time peace, the lands inhabited.
People will travel safely through the sky, land, sea and wave,
Then wars will break out anew.

Les fleaux passes diminue le monde,
Long-temps la paix, terres inhabitees.
Seur marchera par le ciel, terre, mer et onde,
Puis de nouveau les guerres suscitees. (1.63)

Reference to *"mer et onde,"* or *"sea and wave"* is not redundant: ships pass through the wave, submarines through the sea. Observe that mention in the third line to travel by air is casual, almost blase. Nostradamus does not single out air travel as something to wonder at Such sights were so common to his visions that he expresses no more surprise at them than we do. Quite typical of the man, whose prophecies so seldom show feeling of wonder.

In a quatrain which refers to some coming leader of Italy, the seer says:

The armaments will fight in the sky a long time,
The tree fallen in the midst of the city,
Vermin, mange, sword, firebrand in his face,
Then the monarch of Adria will succumb.

Les armes batre au ciel longue saison
L'arbre au milieu de la cite tombe:

> *Verbin rogne, glaive, en face tison.*
> *Lors le monarque d'Hadrie succumbe.*

The lines may concern an event in Armageddon. Some believe "the tree" means the Church.

Two other quatrains foretell air warfare.

> A great king of terror will descend from the skies,
> The year 1999, seventh month,
> To resuscitate the great king of Angolmois,
> Around this time Mars will reign for the good cause.

> *L'an mil neuf cent nonante neuf sept mois,*
> *Du ciel viendra un grand roi d'effrayeur,*
> *Ressusciter le grand roi d'angoulmois;*
> *Avant, apres, regner Mars par bonheur.* (10.72)

In this quatrain Nostradamus speaks as though the king of terror comes from a point of origin other than earth. *If so,* Mars may mean the planet as well as war.

In the following quatrain "Oriental" refers to the near, not far East. The term Orient means East in French, and the appearance of the word in the quatrains always indicates a Near East situation.

> The Oriental will leave his seat,
> He will pass the Apennines to see France:
> And will strike everyone with his rod.
> He will pierce through the sky, the waters and snow,

> *L'Oriental sortira de son siege,*
> *Passer les monts Apennons voir la Gaule:*
> *Transpercera le ciel, les eaux & neige,*
> *Et un chacun frappera de sa gaule.* (2.29)

THE MONTGOLFIER BALLOON

But one of the most amazing prophecies of the French seer is the quatrain in which he actually names the inventor of the balloon, the celebrated French scientist, Joseph Michael Montgolfier. One of the earliest uses the Montgolfier balloon was put to was military. As the Montgolfier was open at the bottom to let in the air, a man in the look-out basket was near the hole when warning the army. The power of his prophecy may be proven by experiment: show the quatrain to someone who has never heard of Montgolfier and he will be unable to make head or tail of the second line. But explain the name and he will understand the passage.

> There will go from Mont Gaulfier and Aventine
> One who from the hole will warn the army.
> The booty will be taken from between two rocks,
> The renown of Sextus the corner-stone will fail.

> *Istra de mont Gaulfier et Aventin,*
> *Qui par le trou advertira l'armee.*
> *Entre deux rocs sera prins le butin,*
> *De Sext. mansol faillir la renommee.* (5.57)

Mont Gaulfier and Montgolfier are one and the same name. In French *au* is pronounced ao; and encyclopaedias list this name once only. This quatrain is beyond the batting-average of chance. If mont-Gaulfier is not a prediction of the Montgolfier balloon the likelihood that anything else in the stanza will bear any possible relation to the celebrated name or the period will be very remote. Yet line two is sun-clear when read with line one — but makes no sense at all without it. Line four mentions a Pope who was an exact contemporary of Montgolfier and his balloon. He was Pius the *Sixth*. And note this: from the time of the prophet until the present, there has not been another Pope in the Holy Sea (Aventine) with that number attached to his name. And in the lives of the Pontiffs his fate stands out easily as one of the most tragic. In the days following the Terror his palace was pillaged by the Red Armies of the Revolution, and he himself carried off to France, where he died. Thus did Nostradamus not only name the balloon and describe a use of it, but even forecast the period when it would appear in the world.

OTHER WEAPONS

Other weapons foreseen by Nostradamus are flame-throwing tanks, used in World War II against his compatriots (see page 125).

Nostradamus foresaw bombs capable of destroying an entire city.

> Live fire will be put in globes, hidden death,
> Horrible, frightful.
> By night the fleet will reduce the city to rubble,
> The city on fire, the enemy indulgent.

> *Sera laisse feu vif, mort cache,*
> *Dedans les globes horrible espouvantable.*
> *De nuict a classe cite en poudre lasche,*
> *La cite a feu, l'ennemi favorable.* (5.8)

Whenever Nostradamus, without qualification, states "the city" he means his beloved Paris. Many are the prophecies in French of the destruction of the French capital. Nostradamus' is simply one more. Are these bombs atomic? Whatever they are they cause so much horrible destruction that even the enemy takes pity and becomes "indulgent."

In the following quatrain the great motor referred to, not yet on the market, may well be atomic-powered:

> After a great human exhaustion a greater makes ready,
> The great motor renovates the centuries:
> Plague blood, milk, famine, iron and pestilence,
> In the sky fire seen, long running spark.

> *Apres grand troche humain plus grand s'appreste*
> *Le grand moteur les ciecles renouvelle:*
> *Playe sang, laict, famine, fer & peste,*
> *Au ciel veu feu, courant longue estincell.* (2.46)

The Life Magazine photographs of the famous Sputnik showed a long, running spark. The "plague blood, milk," may have met partial fulfillment with the discovery in England of contaminated milk. As for the first line of the quatrain, we may wonder if today is intermission time between two great human exhaustions.

In closing these comments on the French seer's forecasts of modern inventions mention should be made of his prediction of the use of coal-gas:

> White coal will be driven from black,
> Made prisoner . . .

> *Le charbon blanc du noir sera chasse,*
> *Prisonier fait . . .* (4.85)

Had Nostradamus' inspiration taken another form, he might have invented any of these things himself. Through that prayer which he so relied on to heighten his prophetic spirit, all knowledge is possible.

OUR NEAR FUTURE

THOUGH WAR-CLOUDS HAVE LOWERED ON THE HORIZON, DARK AND UGLY, and may again, there will be no more major wars for some years to come.

This is not to say that Nostradamus and the other great prophets promise an absence of war forever — many unfulfilled prophecies concern war at its worst, and Armageddon is still to come according to the Bible — but it does mean that the world will not see another global conflict for a period of approximately twelve to fifteen years or so. This information is gained by a careful collation of the most authentic written revelations from different ages and a deduction therefrom of the time element of the most important events to come.

Let us see, from the 16th century seer, the prophet-physician Nostradamus, how the deduction is arrived at. In one of his quatrains, or four-line verse prophecies, he says:

> The year 1999, seventh month,
> A great king of terror will descend from the skies,
> To resuscitate the great king of Angolmois,
> Around this time Mars will reign for the good cause.

> *L'an mil neuf cent nonante neuf sept mois,*
> *Du ciel viendra un grand roi de'effrayeur,*
> *Ressusciter le grand roi d'Angoulmois;*
> *Avant, apres, regner Mars par bonheur.* (10.72)

In this remarkable quatrain — remarkable because Nostradamus not only mentions air-warfare but places it in the 20th century — we see that Armageddon is on in 1999. Mars here obviously signifies war. Its beneficent aspect — "for the good cause" — means that the war is nearly over, with victory on the side of right, i.e., those fighting for "the good cause." (The original French reads "bonheur," which can mean *good cause, good time, or happiness.*) Now, according to Pyramid prophecy, the millennial dawn is due in 2001. So if Armageddon is nearly over in 1999, and over by 2001, its actual termination should be 2000 A.D. From this we deduct 27 years, for Nostradamus says elsewhere, referring to the coming Arab conqueror and the troubles he brings:

> The third Antichrist, soon annhilated,
> But his bloody war will last twenty-seven years.
>
> *L'Antechrist trois bientot annichilez,*
> *Vingt & sept ans sang durera sa guerre . . .* (8.77)

Subtracting 27 from 2000 gives us 1973 for the beginning of the great conflict between good and evil, and 1973 is 12 years away.

Must these things be? Can we not have peace without war at all? It would be pleasant to think so, but honesty compels the interpreter of prophecy to admit that even according to the Bible, the most spiritual book in the world, Armageddon has not yet been fought and won. No matter how metaphysical an interpreter of written revelations is, no matter how clearly he realizes the ultimate unreality of evil, and the omnipotence and omnipresence of God, he must try to tell the complete human story, and like Joseph of Egypt, foretell the lean years as well as the fat. The Hebrew Provider, he who saw symbols in stars, moon and sun, and who read aright strange dreams that even the most noted scryers of Pharaoh's land could not, even he was not so spiritual as to be able to unsee the evil; but he did the next best thing: he brought the foreshadowed ills to the light of intelligence and provided against them. It had been said that the evil that has been found out is two-thirds destroyed. And prophecy assists in the finding it out.

Peace pure and undefiled will not be a suddenly settled thing. The Kingdom of God cometh not with observation. Peace must be worked for and won. Its structure must be built brick by brick.

War aftermaths are confused periods. In the following prophecy, which I first interpreted and applied to the post-war period in my *New Nostradamus*, published in 1944, the great seer describes a world condition that has now arrived:

There will be peace, the union, and the change,
Estates, offices, low high and high put very low.
The journey prepared the first fruit, torment,
War to cease, civilian accusations, debates.

Paix, union sera & changement,
Estats, Offices, bas hault, & hault bien bas.
Dresser voyage, le fruict premier, torment,
Guerre cesser, civils proces, debats. (9.66)

Since World War II there have been many civilian accusations and debates often at fever pitch, both within the frail framework of the United Nations and without. These days are not over.

A part of the prophecy remains to be fulfilled. The great "union" has not yet taken place, nor "the change," which will *include* geographical changes wrought by nature, cataclysms due any time now. "The first fruit" regards the setting up of a workable plan for Anglo-American federation, and "the journey prepared" apparently has reference to a trip by an American leader to effect that purpose, a trip to Europe somewhat after the style of the post-war journey made by Wilson — but a journey with better success. Who the journey will be made by cannot now be known, but there are prophetic indications that part of the Anglo-American plan for "the union" will be formulated by no less a person than Sir Anthony Eden, who may at that time again be Prime Minister of Britain. His knowledge of Arabic and of Arabic affairs will make him a most useful and desirable public servant in a world of constantly increasing Moslem might. It is here worthy of remark that in G. K. Chesterton's prophetic novel, "The Return of Don Quixote," written at the turn of the century, the Golden Age of Saturn ushered in after labor-throes boasts a British Prime Minister named Lord Eden. As this Golden Age is the period of the Great Restoration — as Bacon called it, *Magna Instauratio* the name EDEN is highly significant.

The Golden Age is nearer than the Millennium, in fact, very near indeed. The Kingdom of God is set up after a period of turmoil that is due within the next two years in the two major Anglo-Saxon lands. The Kingdom is symbolized in Scandinavian mythology as the World Tree of Yggdrasil (Israel), which is to grow and spread, and cover the earth. But in the process of spreading it meets with opposition from the forces of evil. This conflict culminates in Armageddon, and the Kingdom is crucified. But like its Founder, it is resurrected, and its resurrection is the Millennium, or the thousand years of Peace. We are today living in the period that is to usher in the glorious Age of Saturn, the Stone Kingdom of Bible prophecy.

The new period will show, as one of its signs, the decline of England as an Imperial World Power. Nostradamus writes:

> The Great Empire will be by England,
> Great forces will pass by land and sea,
> The all-powerful for more than three hundred years;
> The Portuguese will not be pleased with it.

> *Le grand empire sera par Angleterre,*
> *Le Pempotan* des ans de plus de trois cent ans*
> *Grandes copies passer par mer et terre,*
> *Les Lusitans s'en seront pas contens.* (10.100)

This is the last of "the thousand prophecies" of Nostradamus. It has been fearfully interpreted as a prediction of the downfall of England. Why? There is no mention made here of war, no mention of defeat, no mention even of decline. Nostradamus says simply that after more than three hundred years England will no longer be all-powerful. This will be true if England joins an Anglo-Saxon or a world federation. It will be true if America becomes more powerful than she. It may be true now. Already a prime minister of England has stated the United States is the most powerful nation in the world.

The *Britannica* dates the British Empire from 1583. At that time the Portuguese possessed an empire of their own, with a powerful navy. But towards the end of the sevententh century the picture was reversed. England was becoming the mistress of the seas, while the power of the Portuguese was swiftly declining. This could not have pleased them.

It is worthy of note that when Nostradamus penned this prophecy England was just another nation. She was not an Empire, she was not supreme on the seas, and the Armada was waiting to be defeated.

Another Nostradamian prophecy on England, though unlikely-looking at the moment, may belong to the near future:

> Within the Isles a very horrible tumult,
> Nothing will be heard but a clashing of factions,
> The harm wrought by the brigands will be so great
> That the nation will have to take its place in the great league.

---

* *Tan* "all" and *Totens*, "powerful."

Dedans les isles si horrible tumulte,
Rien on n'orra qu'une bellique brigue,
Tant grand sera des proditeurs l'insulte,
Qu'on se viendra ranger a la grand ligue. (2.100)

Nostradamus gives glimpses of a troubled picture in the near future, a period of chemicalization. But that near future will usher in the Golden Age, of which the next quatrain relates the beginning:

There will be a head of London from the government of America
The Island of Scotland, he will pave you with ice;
They will have Reb for King, a very false Antichrist,
Who will put them all in an uproar.

Le chef de Londres par regne l'Americh,
L'Isle d'Ecosse t'empiera par gelee;
Roy Reb auront, un si faux Antechrist,
Qui les mettra trestous dans la meslee. (10.66)

The first line of this prophecy indicates Anglo-American Union, and is remarkable for the fact that when it was penned there was no government of America, for this land was a howling wilderness. Nor was America associated with England in any way, for the first colonists had not at that time been so much as sent over. Nostradamus frequently indulges in such amazing lines, using casually expressions like "Great Britain, comprising England," "the Empire of England," "the government of America" at a time when they were not realities.

"The island of Scotland" apparently suggests the nationality of the London head "from the government of America." "He will pave you with ice," may refer to a Puritanical regime, with its attendant "blue laws," or it may have a more literal meaning which time only can make clear.

When we read prophecies on the coming of "Antichrist," we should remember that the seer, no matter how genuine his ability, may personally hold views at variance with those of another seer describing the same picture. According to some scryers the Era about to begin is the wonderful Age of Saturn, according to others it is the time of Antichrist. Analysis of the prophecies requires great care and discernment. The point of view of the seer must be taken into consideration. Some seers — genuine seers — actually see the Scripture-described Kingdom of God on earth, yet so dislike what they see that they denominate it the reign of Antichrist, because the picture that presents itself to their vision is one in which all religions live side by side in peace and harmony. These men do not see their own particular brand of religion conquering — but only co-existing with the others — and such a state of affairs is to them anathema, hence anti-Christian. Genuine ability to see the future, therefore, does not always include ability to assess the future.

Nostradamus is a case in point. In this "Union Now" quatrain, he describes the head of London from the government of America as "a very false Antichrist." Now the Bible says that in the latter days "false Christs" will arise. But what is "a false Antichrist?" Of course, Nostradamus may mean by false Antichrist an Antichrist who is simply false, in contradistinction to one who is cruel or tyrannical. False, that is, from the point of view of the seer, who was a devout Royalist and Catholic of Renaissance France. Or he may mean someone who is falsely considered Antichrist. At any rate, the *judgment* of Nostradamus aside — and he rarely judges, merely reports — the picture he reveals is that of a federal union between the two great English-speaking democracies, headed by a president who appears to be puritanical and in some way associated with "the isle of Scotland." This union should be a reality before Armageddon.

In essence, this prophecy is in harmony with the Bible prophecies that in the latter days the whole house of Israel — which includes not only the Jews but the multitudinous Anglo-Saxon-Celtic peoples, the so-called Lost Tribes, will be governed by the House of Joseph under "David," who is to be elected by the people. The House of Joseph is made up of Ephraim (Britain) and Manasseh (America).

Such a union will be. The representative emblems or coats of arms of the two nations embed that future fact in their insignia. The British arms carry the Harp of David, the American "arms" the "Star of David." Look at our American seal, portrayed on our dollar bills, and you will see above the Eagle's head thirteen stars formed in such way as to constitute the six-pointed *Mogen Dovid*. Federation will unite both Star and Harp.

The immediate sign of the near approach of the New Order of the Ages is the discovery of atomic power. Just before this day, so Matthew informs us:

"THE POWERS OF THE HEAVENS SHALL BE SHAKEN."

In the original Greek the word "heavens" is Ourania, which is the word from which we derive Uranium, the metal, and the planet of division — symbolizing the two-edged sword of truth. Re-reading the passage, and leaving this one word in its original form, we get:

"THE POWERS OF OURANIA SHALL BE SHAKEN."

To get atomic power we shake Uranium. Now let us read the passage even more literally:

The powers of Uranium shall be shaken: And then shall appear the sign of the Son of man in heaven.

This prophecy is not referring to Jesus Christ, for the Bible explicitly says, "I will send you Elijah the prophet before the coming of the great and dreadful day of the Lord" . . . and . . . "Elijah shall *first* come and restore all things." And certainly, things are at present very far from being restored!

"There is a tradition extant," says Ritter Brown, "among the Indians of the Southwest, extending from Arizona to the Isthmus of Panama, to the effect that Montezuma will one day return on the back of an Eagle, wearing a golden crown, and rule the land once more; typifing the return of the Messiah and the rebirth and renewal of the race."

ADDENDUM

PREDICTIONS BY LOUIS XVI

T HE following predictions, made by the King of France, are not
transcendent, like those of Nostradamus, but they bear an unusual
instinctive quality in their accuracy.

To the Prince de Conde.

October, 1791.

My Cousin,

In vain I have intimated to my brothers how much
those armed assemblies on the banks of the Rhine are contrary
to sound policy, the interests of the exiled French, and my
own cause. They still persist in their resolutions of attack,
threaten us with foreigners, and oppose them to Frenchmen
led astray. This conduct fills me with sorrow, and must pro-
duce the most disastrous consequences: it will perpetuate
hatred, excite vengeance, and deprive me of all means of conci-
liation. The moment that hostilities begin, you may be assured
that all return into France will be impossible; emigration will
become a state-crime: those will then be attacked as criminals,
who now are only victims; and Frenchmen, whom violence had
forced to fly, will be considered as traitors, who sought to
lacerate the bosom of their country. This re-union of emigrants,
which will never obtain my approbation, multiplies a hundred-
fold the forces of my enemies. They persist in considering me
as the soul of your preparations; the Austrian committee,
directed by the genius of the queen, encouraged by my approbation, and who retain you on the banks of the Rhine.
They cry, to Arms: their agents, well instructed, spread themselves in the streets, in the public squares, under the windows

of my palace; and every day they sound in my ear the funeral
cry of "War! war!" I am affrighted at their tenacious obstinacy, their fury, their cries of rage. What madmen! they
wish for war! Ah! if ever the signal were given, it would be
a long and cruel contest: having no other object than vengeance and hatred, it would become barbarous. O God! pre-
serve France from this fatal scourge! let not those homicide
yells be heard! If I must descend from the throne, mount the
scaffold where Charles the First was immolated, and abandon
all that is dear to me on earth, I am ready —but no war! no
war!

Nevertheless the noise of your preparations has reached
me . . . You, my cousin, who are desirous of uniting glory
and duty — you, whom the emigrants consider as their father
and their chief, and I myself esteem as a loyal and magnanimous prince — oppose, I conjure you, the wild projects of
the French assembled around your person; make known to
them the danger; oppose my will, my counsels, even my pray-
ers, to this valor inflamed by injustice, misfortune, and in-
juries. Let us yet dare to hope: the storm may pass away;
happier times may be in reserve for us. I stand in need of
hope, and of learning that you are docile to my voice, in order
to enjoy the moment of happiness.

Louis.

Helen Maria Williams, editor of King Louis' letters, comments on the above: "The Prince of Conde remained inexor-
able. The conquest of France was an object too seducing to
yield to considerations of this nature; and the magnanimity,
the loyalty, and the glory, with which the king compliments his
cousin, in order to flatter him into obedience, the prince
deemed more chivalrously evinced by remaining, what the
king styles him, the 'father and chief' of the emigrants.

To Monsieur

April 26, 1792

. . . I may undergo the fate of Charles the First, because,
when the barriers of justice are broken down, there remains
no more security for him who fills the throne, than for him
who aspires to occupy his place. When the tempest has shattered the vessel, nothing remains for the passenger but the

courage of resignation: and such is nearly my position. Farewell, my dear brother! The dangers I am made to fear shall never have any influence on what I owe to myself as king, and as the chief of one of the first nations of the world.

But the brothers of Louis continued their agitation for war, till they got it. They paid no attention to the pleas of the King, considering him — so they pretended to think — no more than a puppet mouthing the opinions of his captors.

Helen Maria Williams comments: "Letters commanding them to return were delivered to their address at Coblentz, by the French ambassador . . . Under pretence that their titles had been omitted, both assured the king that they hesitated to open his letters, and, persuaded that he was still in moral and physical captivity at Paris, both declared that they would pay respect neither to his entreaties nor his orders. Louis Stanislas Xavier was dissatisfied that his brother had not called him *Monsieur;* and Charles Philippe, that the king had not called him *brother.* Thus sported those idle personages with the feelings and situation of the unhappy monarch, till they succeeded in carrying into execution their hostile purposes to France, which ended, as was predicted by the king, in the total defeat of all their hopes, after causing the overthrow of the throne, of which they affected to appear the bulwark, and bringing the unhappy victim of their petulance and obstinacy to the scaffold." It may also be observed that the brothers' allies, all devout in their royalism, were not in the least concerned with the individual lives of the royal family of France, but only with the principle of royalism. Conquering France, they could set up one of Louis' brothers as king if the Republicans in revenge destroyed the rightful rulers. Stefan Zweig comments acidly: "If, thanks to their (the brothers') machinations, Louis XVI, Marie Antoinette, and (it was to be hoped likewise) the little Dauphin should perish — perhaps after becoming in name Louis XVII — so much the better." Writing from Brussels, Count Fersen said: "There has been the most unseemly joy manifested because the King was taken prisoner; the Count of Artois is positively radiant."